CW01238722

PUTTING OUT THE FIRE

YOUR UNIQUE ROLE IN BRINGING JEWS CLOSER TO TORAH

AHARON UNGAR

First published 2007
Copyright © 2007 by Aharon Ungar
ISBN 978-1-56871-456-1

All rights reserved

No part of this publication may be translated, reproduced, stored in a retrieval system, or transmitted in any form or by any means, electronic, mechanical, photocopying, recording, or otherwise, without prior permission in writing from both the copyright holder and the publisher.

Published by:
TARGUM PRESS, INC.
22700 W. Eleven Mile Rd.
Southfield, MI 48034
E-mail: targum@targum.com
Fax: 888-298-9992
www.targum.com

Distributed by:
FELDHEIM PUBLISHERS
208 Airport Executive Park
Nanuet, NY 10954

Printing plates by Frank, Jerusalem
Printed in Israel by Chish

רב נח אורלווק
סורוצקין 51, דירה 2
ירושלים

בסייעתא דשמיא
ירושלים
אור ל-י״ז חשוון תשס״ח

After having read Rabbi Aharon Ungar's manuscript, *Putting Out the Fire*, I feel that it is an important vehicle for giving us insights into two vital areas of life, both as an individual Jew and as proud member of כלל ישראל.

Firstly, it impresses upon the reader the urgent need for those who have received the gift of Torah knowledge and are privileged to lead a Torah life, to help bring others, who have not been privileged to have this, to taste the wonderful taste of Torah and be drawn close to their heritage. The author shows, in a uniquely positive way, how each individual can be of inestimable value in bringing people close to Torah, and clearing up misconceptions about Torah Jews.

Secondly, this book is full of sensitivity, and reading it thoughtfully will enrich the private lives of the readers, teaching them the principles of caring for and listening to and building bridges to those that are closest to them.

May this book receive the attention that it so richly deserves.

With wishes for much ברכה והצלחה.

Noach Orlowek

HaRav HaGaon Rav Chaim Pinchus Sheinberg

הנני מצטרף לדברי הנ״ל, הרב הגאון רב נח, שמתלמידי המובהקים שלי. הנני מברך את המחבר שיזכה לקרב אחינו בני ישראל לאביהם שבשמים, ולהגדיל תורה ולהאדירה מתוך מנוחת הנפש והרחבת הדעת.

הרב הגאון ר' חיים פנחס שיינברג

Rabbi Noach Orlowek, 51 Sorotzkin, Apt. 2, Jerusalem

Rabbi Zev Leff

Rabbi of Moshav Matityahu
Rosh HaYeshiva—Yeshiva Gedola Matityahu

הרב זאב לף

בס"ד

מרא דאתרא מושב מתתיהו
ראש הישיבה—ישיבה גדולה מתתיהו

D.N. Modiin 71917   Tel: 08–976–1138 טל'   Fax: 08–976–5326 פקס'   ד.נ. מודיעין 71917

Dear Friends,

I have read the manuscript of "Putting Out the Fire" – your unique role in bringing Jews closer to Torah by Rabbi Aharon Ungar. The message Rabbi Ungar delivers is a very important one. This is evident from the many sources he quotes from Gedolei Yisroel who exhort the rank and file of Torah Jewry to actively be involved in Kiruv Rechokim, drawing our estranged brethren closer to Torah.

Rabbi Ungar offers words of encouragement and practical advice as to how exactly everyone can find their specific niche in this crucial pursuit.

The perfection of Klal Yisroel and hence the world depends on all Jews being united as active subjects in G-d's kingdom. Hence, the Rabbis exhort us to be disciples of Aharon Hakohen, who was the representative of the Jewish people before G-d and who carried the names of the Jewish people on his heart. This is achieved by loving shalom – perfection and pursuing perfection, loving all of G-d's creations and striving to bring them closer to Torah.

This book will serve as an excellent handbook and valuable resource guide for this great undertaking.

I commend Rabbi Ungar for his efforts. May Hashem grant him the ability to continue to merit the community with other books and projects. May we soon see the day when the entire world be filled with knowledge of Hashem as the waters cover the sea.

With Torah blessings,

Rabbi Zev Leff

Rabbi Yitzchak Berkovits
Sanhedria HaMurchevet 113/27
Jerusalem, Israel 97707
02-5813847

יצחק שמואל הלוי ברקוביץ
ראש רשת כוללים ליעת הצדק
סנהדרי״ה המורחבת 113/27
ירושלם ת״ו

BsD Yerushalayim
21 Cheshvan 5768

In the struggle to protect authentic Judaism from the forces of secularism, Torah-true Jewry was forced to concentrate its efforts on building and insulating itself from outside influences - to the point of writing off our non-observant brethren.

Today's situation is very different to that of not so long ago. The Torah world has B"H grown, while the apikorsus of old has dissolved into sheer ignorance. Those who reach out are greeted with a sincere thirst for real Torah, yet so many of us are still living with attitudes from the past and are reluctant to get involved.

This work was intended to appeal to the sechel hayashar of the G-d fearing Jew and generate within him a shift in mindset and a desire to join the struggle for kvod Shamayim. The argument is presented well and is quite convincing. The author's practical advice shows how kiruv is doable even without formal training or experience.

I would only add that the most powerful of all arguments in favor of kiruv rechokim are the thousands of wonderful baalei teshuva in our midst - individuals and families of the highest caliber who have embraced Torah with sincerity and mesiras nefesh. Were it not for the yechidim who raised the banner of kiruv before it became socially accepted, so many talmidei chachamim and yirei shamayim among us would have been left to live a live devoid of all ruchnius. Who knows how many elevated yiddishe' neshamos are out there waiting to be brought home to Torah!

May this work be successful at inspiring more and more of us to stand up and be counted in the campaign to restore Klal Yisrael to its position as mamleches kohanim v'goi kadosh.

בברכת התורה,

יצחק ברקוביץ

PUTTING OUT THE FIRE

At an Agudath Israel convention in Europe in the 1920s, the elderly Chofetz Chaim, Rav Yisrael Meir Kagan, used his time at the podium to tell the audience of legendary Torah figures that everybody has an obligation to invest effort in *kiruv rechokim*. Later in the program, the Chofetz Chaim asked if he could speak again. With a roster full of luminaries, another slot was not easy to arrange, but the other speakers shortened their remarks in deference to the Chofetz Chaim, and he returned to the podium. What was the burning message that he insisted on delivering?

"I heard that after I spoke, people were saying, 'The Chofetz Chaim didn't mean me. I'm not talented enough, I'm not smart enough. Obviously when he said "everybody," he didn't mean me.' So I want to tell you a story," the Chofetz Chaim told the crowd.

"Once there was a nobleman who owned a large tract of land with many villages. One day, he was traveling around his land and he stopped at a village. A villager gave him a drink of water. He took one sip and immediately spat it out in disgust.

" 'This water is terrible!' he said. 'It has sand in it.'

" 'The villagers responded, 'That's how the water is here.'

"The nobleman warned them, 'You can't drink this. It's not healthy. From now on, before you use this water, it has to be filtered.'

"Weeks later, the nobleman was looking out at the horizon and he saw that the village he had visited was on fire. He quickly saddled his horse and rode as fast as he could to the village. When he finally arrived, he saw everyone standing idly as the fire blazed. 'Why don't you put out the fire?' he demanded. 'Why are you just standing there?'

" 'We are waiting for the water to be filtered,' one villager informed him.

" 'For drinking, you need filtered water!' the nobleman exclaimed. 'This is a fire! To put out a fire, you use whatever water you have!'

"There is a raging fire that is destroying *Klal Yisrael*… We have to put it out!"

THE GEDOLIM TALK ABOUT KIRUV

HaRav Shmuel Kamenetsky, shlita
"In giving *chizuk* to a non-*frum* Jew, the *frum* person is blessed with much *Siyata d'Shmaya* and is tremendously *mischazek* himself."

The Novominsker Rebbe, HaRav Yaakov Perlow, shlita
"*Kiruv rechokim*, I believe, is the mitzvah of our generation."

HaRav Moshe Feinstein, zt"l
"Just as one is *mechuyav* to give a tenth of one's income, so one is *mechuyav* to give a tenth of one's time to teaching others..."

HaRav Yisrael Meir Kagan (The Chofetz Chaim), zt"l
"In truth, when one ponders and understands the status of Torah in recent years, and how it has fallen so much in today's world, then the obligation on every *baal Torah* who has learned…is that much greater to fight the battles of Torah…

"The war being fought against G-d and His Torah is a continuous threat, worsening daily. Therefore it is incumbent upon every person who knows even a little Torah to do all that he can. If he just knows *Chumash*, he must put together a learning group and teach them *Chumash*. If he knows *Mishnah*, he should teach *Mishnah*...

"One who has learned a few years in yeshiva, and has thus acquired much Torah knowledge, must never say he is exempt. Rather, he is obligated to go out to the battlefield and lead as many Torah learning groups as he can. Not only that, but he is more obligated than anyone else. It is up to him to urge, awaken and assemble the congregation and show them 'the right way'...and through this the honor of Hashem will multiply throughout the world. A war like this one is not a *milchemes reshus*, an optional war; rather, it is a *milchemes mitzvah*, a positive commandment in which everyone is obligated to shoulder a portion..."

HaRav Eliezer Menachem Mann Shach, zt"l
"If one man can murder six million Jews, certainly one man can save six million Jews."

HaRav Shlomo Wolbe, zt"l
"If every *yungerman* would contribute a portion of his time to *kiruv rechokim*, every single Jew in Eretz Yisrael will be brought back to the ways of the Torah."

CONTENTS

Dedication xiii
Acknowledgements xix
Foreword xxv
Introduction xxxi

Chapter 1: Why Kiruv? 1
Chapter 2: Is Kiruv for You? 9
Chapter 3: Practical Kiruv 27
Chapter 4: Developing Relationships 40
Chapter 5: Effective First Steps 50
Chapter 6: Helping Jews Find G-d in Shul ... 61
Chapter 7: Three Unbelievable Programs
   You Can Join, Emulate or Support 70
Chapter 8: 99 Kiruv Ideas 92
Chapter 9: Project Inspire 107
Chapter 10: The Vision 116
Chapter 11: Conclusion 119

Appendix: Kiruv Resources 125

DEDICATION

"If it wasn't for your father," my friend's father said to me a few years ago when I visited Atlanta, Georgia, "I would have none of this. The fact that my wife and I are religious, that all of our children went to yeshiva and our grandchildren are growing up as *ehrliche Yidden*, is all because of your father."

I had no idea. This man's son had been one of my closest friends for as long as I can remember, and now, as an adult visiting Atlanta, I found out that their family was *mekarev* by my father, Rabbi Cantor Robert Ungar.

"And you know what," he continued, "we're not the only ones. There are many of us," and he started naming names, many of whom were now among the leading "original" *frum* families in Atlanta. I truly had no idea. Here before me was living proof of the Rabbinic dictum that if one saves one life, it is as though he saved the entire world. My father was *mekarev* numerous individuals and couples who built religious families and now have religious children and grandchildren. New worlds had been created.

Over the last few years, I began to think more and more about the power of *kiruv*. Although my father passed away, he lives on in all of these families and their descendants; and he shares in all of their mitzvos and *limud haTorah*.

Growing up, we virtually never had a Shabbos lunch without guests, and most of them were not religious. Some were regulars who came every few weeks, others periodically, and there was one woman who came every week. There were questions, answers, explanations, discussions, stories and lots of *zemiros*.

In retrospect, it seems that most of my parents' friends were not religious at the time. Today, many of those families are. My parents understood that *kiruv* meant developing relationships and showing a love for a Torah way of life through example. My father found unique ways of involving others and took advantage of his many talents to build those relationships. Some examples:

My father was an excellent ballplayer. He had been drafted to play Major League Baseball by the New York Giants when a scout saw him play a sandlot pick-up game, but he turned it down because he would have to play on Shabbos. So on Lag BaOmer he would make sure to invite loads of people to the shul softball game. People laughed when the overweight chazan got up to bat, and those who had never been there before would teasingly move in from the outfield — until the next pitch when the ball went flying over their heads. People would see a new side to him and realize that he was approachable and normal, just like they were.

Sometimes my father would invite a guest to play

Dedication

a friendly game of Ping-Pong. The initial volleys were no big deal, but then, all of sudden, my father would slam the ball. After that there was no turning back. Very few people knew that, in his youth, my father had been the Ping-Pong champion of the State of Connecticut. Again, now he wasn't the cantor or the rabbi; he was somebody they could get to know and hang out with.

My father was doing *kiruv* before it had a name, even in the middle of the Korean War. My father was, for a time, the only Jewish chaplain in Korea. I guess that made him the chief rabbi of Korea! When it was time for Pesach, my father organized massive Seders for thousands of Jewish troops. He arranged for a train, nicknamed the *Seder Express*, to travel from one end of the country to the other to pick up all the Jewish servicemen and bring them to a central location. There they celebrated Pesach together with imported kosher for Pesach matzah, wine, Haggadahs and food provided by the Jewish War Veterans.

To spread his love for *Yiddishkeit*, for many years, in the sixties, my father initiated and hosted what was at the time the only ongoing, weekly Jewish radio program in the southern United States, featuring music, stories and comments. And, indeed, that love was contagious as thousands listened weekly and thereby drew closer to their heritage.

As a pioneer in American *kiruv*, my father published two records. One, combined with a workbook which he designed himself, was the first interactive method to teach oneself how to chant a haftorah with the proper trop. The second, in conjunction with members of his shul, taught bar mitzvah boys, and others, how to lead the Shabbos davening.

Yet with all of these ancillary activities and the many boards of various Jewish institutions in the community that he always served on, Daddy was first and foremost a teacher. His favorite subject was *Pirkei Avos*. When he taught adults, they would forget what was happening outside of that room as they were totally engaged. When he would teach children, they would sit spellbound, waiting, hoping for a story from this master storyteller. He would give numerous *shiurim* on a weekly basis, each one tailored for its particular audience.

When I was a boy, probably about 10 years old, my father asked me what I wanted to do when I grew up. I said I didn't know, but that I wanted to be rich. My father seemed surprised by this answer. Then he asked me, "Well, what would you do if you had a million dollars?" I answered that I would use it to start a company and turn it into ten million and then 100 million dollars. He smiled, and said, "Not me." Now it was my turn to be surprised. I asked, "So what would you do with a million dollars?" He looked me in the eye and answered, "I would invest it carefully, live off the interest, and spend all my time learning and teaching Torah." Little did I know then that even in this seemingly trivial conversation, Daddy was planting a seed and teaching. In fact, that short little interchange may

Dedication

have taught me the most important lesson of my life: Everything that one does must be *l'shem Shamayim*, including striving to become a millionaire.

About thirty years later, I chose to do it Daddy's way. My wife and I sold our business and I retired to the *beis midrash* to learn.

May this book, written in memory of my father, Rabbi Cantor Robert Ungar, HaRav Yisrael ben Shmuel, *z"l*, be a fitting memory to one of such stature, who earned the *Keser Shem Tov* as he fought for Hashem on the front lines of assimilation.

ACKNOWLEDGEMENTS

Baruch shehecheyanu v'kiyemanu v'higiyanu lazman hazeh. Although short, this book was over two years in the making. May it be Hashem's will that it be read and acted upon by hundreds of thousands of Jews.

I would like to thank Rabbi Chaim Hersh and his Rabbinic advisors at the Achim organization, Rabbi Zev Leff and Rabbi Noach Orlowek. As explained in this book, the lecture series offered by Achim provided the initial material for this book. In addition, many of the organization's *maggidei shiur* have given permission for us to video their *shiurim*, for use in future *kiruv* training videos to be shown in shuls across America. In particular, I would like to thank Rabbi Moshe Zeldman for the challenge he posed in the *shiur* that he taught, which led to my undertaking this book.

Of course, I must thank all of the *maggidei shiur* whose material appears throughout these pages. In addition, there were many other people who gave permission, whose material did not make it in to this volume, but which I hope to make available in future books. Each one did not simply say yes, but also gave me tremendous *chizuk* and encouragement that this was a vital message that should be publicized.

My editor, Chana Nestlebaum, was a blessing from Hashem. It was clear from the time I saw her first sample revisions that she had a great talent for digesting and simplifying large volumes of information into succinct sections and distinct points. She took the revisions that I had made on the transcribed *shiurim* and made them eminently more readable and memorable.

Alan Proctor heard about my book and tracked me down. He had never heard of me, nor I him, but we were immediately drawn together as kindred *neshamos*, linked by our common business backgrounds, love for *acheinu kol beis Yisrael* and commitment to sharing *Yiddishkeit* with every last one of them. Alan has been a great sounding board and a major help in introducing me to many of the "movers and shakers" in *kiruv*, from whom I have sought perspective and insight on the *kiruv* movement. Without his feedback and contacts, this book would be much less helpful to the reader.

My mother, Sura D. Ungar, has always been one of my biggest fans. I have so much for which to thank her and my father, Rabbi Cantor Robert Ungar, *z"l*, that I cannot begin to write it here. She taught me that I can accomplish anything I set my mind to doing and to never give up until the last "ping is ponged." Without the *bayis ne'eman b'Yisrael* in which she and my father raised me and my siblings, I doubt I would ever have

Acknowledgements

properly understood *kiruv*. For them, *kiruv* was not a job or a program or a task, it was a way of life. It is that philosophy which I hope pervades this book.

I must also publicly acknowledge the tremendous *hakaras hatov* I have for my two *Rabbeim*, Rabbi Yerucham Bensinger, *Rav* of the Torah V'Emunah *kehilla* of North Miami Beach, Florida, and Rabbi Moshe Meiselman, *Rosh Yeshiva* of Yeshivas Toras Moshe in Yerushalayim. Walking away from an exciting, successful entrepreneurial career to re-enter the *beis midrash* full-time is a very difficult transition. As important and meaningful as learning has always been to me, it is one thing to be *kovei'a itim laTorah*, it is quite another to do it all day. Without their constant *chizuk* and more *chizuk* and then more *chizuk*, I would never have gotten over the hump. The allure of business nearly pulled me back many times. Truly, if not for them, and the warm, patient, knowledgeable *chavrusos* with whom they matched me, my seat in the *beis midrash* would be filled by someone else.

My current and recent *chavrusos*, Rabbis Simcha Bidnick, Aryeh Sokol and Lazer Saposh, deserve my utmost thanks for their patience with my off-the-topic discussions about *kiruv* and my periodic absences from *seder* which resulted from my work on this book. May *Hakadosh Baruch Hu* bless them for their commitment to *limud HaTorah* and the encouragement they constantly have given me; and, most of all, for all that I continue to learn from them.

I must also thank Rabbi David Gorelik who gave

me my first formal, hands-on *kiruv* opportunity when he asked me to tutor *baalei teshuvah* and *geirim* who had come to him for guidance. I didn't think I knew enough to do the job, but he convinced me that I did and assured me that he would be available to answer any questions that might arise. The exhilaration of observing the growth of my students hooked me on *kiruv* for life.

Finally, I would like to thank Yechiel Kahan-Frankl, a very good friend who hung in there with me to the very end. When the final deadline beckoned and there were so many details still to address, he made himself available to help — even staying up with me until 5 a.m.

Above all, I must thank my *eizer kenegdo*, the *eishes chayil* who put up with the many evenings that I hid in my home office typing away. Jennifer is the glue that holds our family together, and nothing would get done in my life without her love, support and organizational skills. To paraphrase Rabbi Akiva, all that I have, much of what I am and most of what I will be is because of her. In addition, I must thank each of my children, Nachum, Yaakov Aryeh, Ariella Tzipora, Akiva Baruch, Esther Tzirel and Yael Bracha. All of them had to give up a lot of personal time with me as I focused so much on getting this book out. Their ongoing patience over two years was a major factor in enabling me to complete this book.

As we are about to go to print, I must add a few more sentences. It is absolutely unheard of to sign a book contract and go to print in about 10 days. Yet due to the wonderful opportunity to distribute this book to all attendees at the upcoming annual convention of Agudath Israel, everybody involved in preparing this book for publication has put everything aside to do exactly that. I do not have the words to express my tremendous *hakaras hatov* to all the people at Global Visions Israel, headed by Chevy (Fleischman) Weiss, and Targum Press, under the direction of Miriam Zakon, Editor-in-Chief. The enthusiasm they bring to their work, their dedication to quality and the importance they ascribe to the message of this book is inspiring and, in my experience, unparalleled.

Similarly, I owe enormous thanks to all of the *Rabbonim*, especially Rabbi Zev Leff, Rabbi Noach Orlowek, and Rabbi Yizchak Berkovits who have made the time to read the manuscript *"al regel achas,"* usually in the wee hours of the night, in order to provide *haskamos* within an impossible schedule of days. In most cases, I had no personal relationship with them prior to this, and yet their superhuman efforts to help me produce a book that would be widely accepted and their demonstrated commitment to serving *Klal Yisrael* was truly humbling.

Even with all the help I received, if there are any errors herein, I accept full responsibility. I ask that any readers who are interested to feel free to share their constructive thoughts with me, both positive and negative. Perhaps, together we will write a new chapter in Jewish history.

Aharon Ungar
aharonungar@gmail.com

FOREWORD
by Rabbi Chanan (Antony) Gordon

I am deeply honored to have been asked to write the foreword to a book whose content addresses the underlying battle cry that has, through clear *hashgachah pratis*, become one of my life goals. In short, to sensitize, educate and then mobilize the untapped and yet highly talented spiritual soldiers that are part of the Orthodox denomination.

The task of the few thousand full-time *kiruv* profes-

Chanan (Antony) Gordon has assumed a leadership role as an *askan* in *klal*-related matters on a national level. Reb Chanan's research article, entitled "Will Your Grandchild Be Jewish?" co-authored by Richard Horowitz (President of Aish HaTorah, North America) received international acclaim and was published in over eight languages in numerous publications. Reb Chanan is a Fulbright Scholar, Sir Abe Bailey Fellow and graduate of the Harvard Law School. Between his many *klal*-related and specifically *kiruv*-oriented commitments, he has worked on Wall Street for the past 13 years and is currently a principle in a hedge fund after leaving Morgan Stanley as a Senior Vice President. Reb Chanan can be contacted at chanan.gordon@lakiruv.com.

sionals, our "permanent force," to dispel the ignorance that permeates the 4,500,000 disenfranchised American Jews is overwhelming. At best, from a purely quantitative statistical perspective, we can win only a small percentage of "battles."

To really win the war against the pernicious effects of assimilation, we have to increase the size of our army even if most of the new recruits remain out of the frontline combat zone. If we can successfully enlist 45,000 members of the Orthodox denomination in America, i.e., just 1 percent of the number of Jews in America that are currently not living a Torah-observant lifestyle, it is my submission that we can win one of the most challenging spiritual wars *Klal Yisrael* has ever faced. Being that there are currently approximately 500,000 "card-carrying members" of the Orthodox community in America, I believe that this goal is realistic and highly achievable.

Koheles teaches us that everything has a season and a time. The Divinely orchestrated sequence of events that led up to my meeting Reb Aharon Ungar, whose insightful research and field studies are so well captured in this book, has made it clear to me that we are at the most auspicious time in Jewish history to "wake the sleeping giant" and mobilize our vibrant Orthodox army to awaken the *pintele Yid* in every Jew.

The high points of the aforementioned sequence of events were as follows:

I was *zocheh* to have been the Chairman of the 2007 AJOP (Association for American Jewish Out-

Foreword

reach Programs) Convention in Baltimore, which is the largest annual gathering of *kiruv* professionals and *askanim* in the world. At the Plenary Session of that AJOP Convention, Rav Aharon Feldman, *shlita*, cited the inter-denominational trans-generational chart that was the highlight of the article that was researched and authored by myself and my esteemed co-author and friend, Richard Horowitz. In his remarks, he was at pains to point out to the capacity audience that in effect all things being equal, if nothing proactive is done, we have 20 years left in America before facing a complete demographic decimation of millions of Jewish *neshamos*.

While 20 years is a blink of an eye considering our 5768-year history, the contagious impact of 45,000 "spiritual foot soldiers" embarking on a 20-year campaign together would surely get the job done. My research into the effect of the viral impact made by successful multi-level marketing companies in less than 20 years convinced me that as long as we have the appropriate ammunition and ability to quantify our success, not only could we succeed, but surely with *Siyata d'Shmaya* we could not fail.

Between 1939 and 1945, when our people experienced the most horrific physical genocide of the 20th century, a few *yichidim*, led by the likes of Mike Tress, formed a *Vaad Hatzolah* to do everything possible to salvage as many *Yiddishe neshamos* as possible. While the holocaust that we are facing today is seductive, painless and ostensibly less graphic, the demographic impact is no less tragic.

There are, however, a number of important differences between the physical holocaust that we experienced during the Second World War and the spiritual holocaust that we are facing today. Firstly, the short time gap between the sounds of the shattering glass on the eve of Kristalnacht in 1938 until the Nazis, *yimach shemam*, began executing the Final Solution caught most organizations flat-footed and unable to develop effective responses.

In stark contrast, today we have the channels in place, and while the fuse is burning fast, if we launch a national grassroots groundswell we have just enough time to succeed.

Secondly, what possible tools and ammunition did we have in hand to fight the death machines established by the Third Reich? A quick perusal of *Putting Out the Fire: Your Unique Role in Bringing Jews Closer to Torah* should make it self-evident that we have the ammunition and the tools to successfully prevail in this war.

Soon after the AJOP Convention I literally pounded the tables at the National Office of Agudath Israel of America to embrace this basic battle cry as the underlying theme at the organization's 85th Annual National Convention. Kudos must go to the likes of Rabbi Shmuel Bloom (Executive Vice President, Agudath Israel) and Rabbi Gedaliah Weinberger (Chairman of the Board of Trustees, Agudath Israel) and all those involved for agreeing to utilize the 2007 Agudath Israel Convention in many ways as a springboard to begin mobilizing the larger army under the theme of

Foreword

"American Jewry at Cliff's Edge — Our Role in Bringing Jews Back to Torah." I am personally grateful to Agudath Israel for having asked me to serve as the Co-Chairman of this historic convention.

In more ways than one, Aharon Ungar's book, *Putting Out the Fire: Your Unique Role in Bringing Jews Closer to Torah*, was the missing piece in the puzzle as we began to plot the best strategies in the Agudath Israel "war room." Consequently, it was my pleasure to present every delegate registered at the 85th Annual National Convention of Agudath Israel of America with a copy of this book which was officially released at the Convention.

When all is said and done, and when the adrenaline of the *hisorerus* of the convention dissipates, this book gives many answers to the many questions that will echo when the curtain falls. We clearly have a *chiyuv* and our *gedolim* are telling us that this is one of the most important mitzvos of our generation but, *lemaysa*, how do I discharge my obligation? How do I get involved? What role can I play to be part of the solution? Reb Aharon's book contains the answers to these questions which will clearly be germane for the next 20 years…until *b'ezras Hashem* we will see the tide of assimilation being contained and reversed by thousands of our estranged brothers and sisters experiencing the beauty of living a true Torah-observant life and the rebuilding of the *Beis Hamikdash* soon in our days.

INTRODUCTION

Standing before a room full of attentive recruits, the riveting speaker spelled out the life-and-death stakes of the war they had volunteered to fight. He described the fearsome enemy — strong, ruthless and, thus far, highly successful. This enemy was abducting Jews from *Klal Yisrael* in astounding numbers and paralyzing their resistance. Wherever it struck, it laid waste to the Jews in its grasp and guaranteed that no new generation would rise up to replace them. Who was this terrible enemy that has been fighting relentlessly for decades against millions of Jews? Assimilation and its inevitable ally, intermarriage.

"This is an enemy that uses tanks and bombs and planes," Rabbi Moshe Zeldman told the crowd. "But what are we shooting with? We are using BB guns."

His stark assessment rang true. Against this massive onslaught, all *Klal Yisrael* had managed to deploy were a few scattered *kiruv* organizations, a few seminars and a few devoted souls who did their best to mount a rescue. The odds were ridiculously slanted in favor of the enemy, not because it was inherently stronger, but because the opposing forces had never meaningfully engaged in the battle.

The program for which Rabbi Zeldman was speaking was an effort to mobilize the ground forces and offer a legitimate fight in the war. The program, Achim, was developed by Rabbi Chaim Hersh, and his wife, Ruthy, who developed and runs the women's division, Aishet, to give *kiruv* training to post-high-school men and women studying in Israel. The goal was to prepare them so that when they would return to their hometowns throughout the world, they would relate to their non-religious neighbors and colleagues in a different way. They would see them as people to whom they could reach out, offer friendship and make an impact. With Hashem's help, they could draw these Jews closer to Torah. Maybe they could even influence their religious friends and relatives to do the same. Thus, the vastly outnumbered forces of formal *kiruv* would have a far-flung, grassroots base of foot soldiers to fill in the immense gaps in the battle lines.

For those who might have thought the battle was already being won — as evidenced by the thousands of *baalei teshuvah* who have become so remarkable a presence over the past few decades — Rabbi Zeldman provided a far more realistic vision. The thousands brought back to Torah through *kiruv* organizations still comprise only a small drop in a raging ocean. Yes, he confirmed, saving one Jewish soul is the equivalent of saving the world, but for every person who finds his Jewish identity, thousands of others are lost each day. "Aish HaTorah will do a seminar, and a hundred people will come," he explained. "Ten will come to follow-up classes, two will come for a Shabbos and one will become *frum*. That's a great thing, but what about the other 99 that came to the seminar? What about the other thousand in the neighborhood and the other hundred thousand in the city that didn't even hear about the seminar because there are not enough people doing *kiruv*?"

What is our generation doing about this tragedy that plays out every day all around us? Can we content ourselves with a few overtaxed *kiruv* groups saving one out of 10,000 lost Jews? "*Hakadosh Baruch Hu* wants all of His children back!" Rabbi Zeldman pleaded. "He didn't put Jews in this world to get lost."

Who will save these Jews if not those who have the education, the background, the understanding of what they are missing in this world and the next? They are the only ones who can help, and they can only do so by finding a place in their hearts for the fate of the rest of *Klal Yisrael*, by caring about Jews who might not even know their Hebrew names or who might not even have one. They have to care that there are Jews who may have no idea of how to daven, how to learn, or how to serve Hashem with any of the hundreds of mitzvos that have been lost to secular Jewry. By opening their hearts, they will find so many ways to reach out to these people in the course of their daily lives, not as professional *kiruv* workers, but as caring fellow Jews. "All I am asking," said Rabbi Zeldman, "is to spend a few minutes once a week thinking about this problem. See if there's a solution we haven't thought of yet." In other words, he urged, each person must make this problem their own.

I was in the audience when Rabbi Zeldman issued this challenge, and it spoke directly to me. As a person with a lot of experience in marketing, I considered this to be the ultimate marketing challenge — one that could change the course of history. I thought about it constantly; I could barely sleep. Finally, after a month of nearly obsessive rumination, an idea came to me that was so obvious and simple. What if I used the Achim model which focuses on students and developed a program for adults to reach out to other adults? It could function like a modified Jewish multi-level marketing organization — a spiritual Amway enterprise. Each person could share his perspectives and knowledge with his friends, while guidance, training and motivation would be provided by those with more experience — *kiruv* professionals. The idea was intriguing.

I sat down and outlined how it might function. Then I wrote an eight-page plan that fleshed out how it might start, grow and be managed, beginning locally, then regionally and finally worldwide. The plan showed that if we could encourage thousands of knowledgeable Jews to sow little seeds of *kiruv*, all of our efforts together would plant so many seeds that whole forests would grow. We could literally change

Introduction

Jewish and world history. Best of all, the resources are already there. We need only to find a way to motivate and guide the masses of people whose involvement is necessary to turn the plan into reality.

This book was written to ignite the spark. It is a call to action, begging the observant community to wake up to the situation unfolding all around us. We live at a turning point in Jewish history. At least one-half of the Jewish population outside of Israel is disappearing and will be completely gone by the time our children are adults. This is not one of those long-term projections that invariably prove wrong; it is a documented demographic trend, and it is happening right now.

The *kiruv* organizations cannot do the job alone. There are not enough *kiruv* professionals, there is not enough money, nor is there enough time for each of them to contact and influence the millions of people who must be reached. The only answer is for each of us to do something.

Even before opening this book, you may have considered becoming more involved in *kiruv*, but something has stood in your way. Perhaps you worried that you wouldn't be able to answer someone's questions, or that you might make a mistake that would turn someone off, or that your own imperfections would make you a faulty role model. Perhaps you cannot imagine fitting another obligation into your schedule. This is exactly why I have researched and written this book — to explain just how easy it is to have a major impact on someone's life, even without great expertise and lots of free time.

Everyone can do something. Some people will love getting into deep conversations about life and meaning. Others who are very uncomfortable with that or exposing themselves or their families to a non-*frum* lifestyle will see that there are many other ways to be involved with *kiruv* without having to do anything they are ill-at-ease with.

The keys are awareness and caring. Someone might ask you a simple, innocent question, such as "Why do Jews wear yarmulkes?" Without an awareness of *kiruv*, you might answer with a joke ("It covers my bald spot.") or by admitting, "I really don't know," with no follow-up offer to find out. With the right awareness and care, however, the interaction would be different. You would see that question as an effort to connect with you as a Jew. You would honor the question and give or get a meaningful answer. You would perhaps ask a follow-up question that would drive the conversation just a drop deeper. There is no set script for turning a Jew on to Judaism. Books, videos, classes and first-hand experiences are all crucial to ultimate success. But invariably the catalyst and the clincher is a person who cared.

All of us come into contact with non-religious people virtually every day. Do you really know them, who they are and what their lives are about? Do they have children, interests, talents? Take the time to make a real, sincere connection. As you will see in the ensuing chapters, everything else flows from there, for the

Introduction

foundation of *kiruv* is simply developing relationships and letting others know you care about them.

It is through this closeness — if you choose to get directly involved — that they have the opportunity to see the beauty of your way of life. Even if you think your life is not particularly inspiring, you cannot imagine how it looks in the eyes of someone who has never sat at a Shabbos table or seen the bustle of a large family or absorbed even one small bit of Torah wisdom. Very often, your non-religious friend will come to want what you have, completely on his own, without the slightest push from you. All you have to do is open that world to him and let him look inside. He will want to learn from you, but only if you let him know you care about him and his life.

For those to whom time is the issue, consider this sobering fact. The churches have a long history of training lay people to convert others to their religion. We have all had encounters with such people — ordinary men and women who are on the alert at all times for the moment when they can introduce their subject to a Jew who might be a colleague or neighbor. One of my former employees regularly tried to initiate theological discussions with me, and even showed me her detailed manual for training lay people to be missionaries to the masses. The materials covered every facet of the process. All she did was come to work every day, but she had her mission burning in her heart, and she used every opportunity to try to accomplish it.

Chazal teach that there is wisdom that can be attained from the other nations of the world, and this missionary paradigm is one that has been successful for centuries. What they have used to snatch Jewish souls, we can use to bring them home. As the following statistics convey starkly, we must act now, or millions more Jews will be lost.

According to studies such as the National Population Study done by Egon Mayer and a National Jewish Population Survey commissioned by the Council of Jewish Federations, as reported in *Mishpacha Magazine* (8.31.05), "At least one-third of all married American Jews are married to a non-Jew. In some communities the number has already reached 50 percent. The studies also show that Jewish children raised in an intermarried household will themselves be much more likely to intermarry than those raised in a home where both parents are Jewish…It should come as no surprise that one million Jewish children, comprising 54 percent of all American-Jewish children under the age of 18, are being raised as non-Jews or with no religion at all."

Worse yet, the traditional Jewish disapproval of intermarriage, which used to exist even among non-religious Jews, has actually turned on its head. According to a study done by the American Jewish Committee on intermarriage, also cited in the same issue of *Mishpacha*, "An amazing 50 percent of the Jews polled in the survey consider opposition to intermarriage to be 'racist.' " It is no wonder that many *kiruv* professionals refer to the current trend as a holocaust — a holocaust of assimilation — painless and sweet, but deadly.

Introduction

This book is a beginning. We have the know-how, techniques and tools, and we have millions of prospects who need what we have to offer them. We just need people to do it. And you don't have to do it alone. You can work with your local Rabbis and *kiruv* professionals or get involved with one of the programs you will read about in this book. All can offer support, motivation and sharing of ideas. Think global, work local. It can be done. By pushing together, we can muster the force to reverse the tide of assimilation, and make this world a place where the *Shechinah* can dwell among us again.

Chapter 1
WHY KIRUV?

We dream of the *Geulah* — that golden, glorious time in our future when we will live completely spiritually centered lives, lives of peace and perfect understanding. In that dream, the Jewish people are redeemed, and we live together in the Land of Israel as one big, loving family with Moshiach as our king. But who is included in that family? Is it all of *Klal Yisrael*, all of our brothers and sisters? Or is it just the tiny fraction of our nation that is Torah observant?

Chazal teach that our sojourn in Mitzrayim is a spiritual template for understanding both our current exile and the *Geulah* that lies ahead. When we examine the lessons learned from that experience and apply them to the current state of American Jewry, then we arrive at a conclusion that has profound implications

---

Adapted from a lecture by Rabbi Yitzchok Lowenbraun, National Director of the Association for Jewish Outreach Programs (AJOP).

for how we view *kiruv*.

When Yaakov began his journey to Mitzrayim, he was gripped with fear that his family would not survive spiritually in that environment. Hashem allayed his concerns, saying *"Do not be afraid of descending to Egypt for I will make you into a great nation there. I will descend with you into Egypt, and it is certain that I will also bring you up…"* But when the time finally came for the Jews to leave Mitzrayim, there seemed to be a troubling dissonance between this promise and what actually happened. According to the *Midrash*, only 20 percent of the people were redeemed, while the remaining 80 percent died during the plague of darkness. As sweet as the redemption from Egypt was, it was bittersweet, for so many Jewish souls, so many generations of Jewish children and grandchildren, so much potential was lost forever.

Why was so large a majority of Jews left behind? The *Midrash* tells us it was because they had cut themselves off from the Jewish future by assimilating into Egyptian culture. They attended the Egyptian cultural events of the day; they even stopped the practice of *bris milah* in order to be indistinguishable from their Egyptian neighbors. Submerged in a polluted society, they fell as far as one can fall into the world of spiritual impurity and still be saved — to the "forty-ninth level of *tumah*."

Against this backdrop, one must ask, "What happened to Hashem's promise to Yaakov that his children would emerge from Egypt?"

The Netziv, Rabbi Naftoli Tzvi Yehudah Berlin, in *Haamek Davar*, on the *pesukim* in *Bereishis* 46:4 and *Shemos* 3:14, provides an answer that contains a chilling message for our time: although Hashem's promise was iron-clad, each individual Jew still had free choice. He could choose to assimilate or to remain distinct from Egyptian society. Redemption was the promise; who and how many would ultimately be redeemed was an entirely different matter, and it was determined not by Hashem, but by the choices made by the people themselves.

Are we destined to lose eighty percent again?

This leaves us with a painful question: If the redemption from Egypt is the template for the coming *Geulah*, does that mean that once again the vast majority of the Jewish people will be left behind in the spiritual wasteland of history? *Geulah* is the promise, but how many will have the privilege to still be a part of *Klal Yisrael* when it finally comes?

Those who work in *kiruv* know that the existing situation in America is not a potential crisis, a looming crisis or an imminent crisis; rather, it is a tidal wave that has already crashed down upon us. There can be little doubt that seven out of 10 American Jews who marry do so with non-Jews, and that in the natural course of events, the vast majority of American Jews will be forever lost to the oblivion of assimilation. Without a seismic shift — a true spiritual earthquake — America is destined to become not only the final resting place for the bodies of millions of Jews who are born, live and die here, but also a vast graveyard for millions of Jewish *neshamos*. This is not what may happen, but exactly what is taking place at a pace that quickens with each passing day.

With regard to American Jewry, the all too horrific question has become: Must we just grab a few life preservers for ourselves and our families while a huge ship filled with millions of Jews goes under, or is it still possible to right the vessel? Is it still possible to enable not just five or 10 percent to be a part of the Jewish future, but 60, 70, or even 100 percent?

Meet the Bernsteins

If we do indeed undertake this massive rescue mission, the first obstacle we face is this: the passengers don't even know their ship is sinking. They don't understand what all the commotion is about. Besides those to whom Judaism has become completely irrelevant, there are many who love Judaism and think of themselves as good Jews. They are proud of their children in Hebrew school, their attendance at Friday night services and their membership in the local Jewish Community Center (JCC). They believe this will provide a Jewish future for their family, but every statistic available shows clearly that it will not. Let's meet one such family and see exactly how they relate to their Jewish identity.

Jeff and Bonnie Bernstein have two children. Jeff is 40 years old and grew up in a suburb of Philadelphia. Jeff's family belonged to a Conservative synagogue, though they only attended services on Yom Kippur and the first day of Rosh Hashana. Jeff's parents wanted him to be a proud Jew, and so they sent him to an afternoon Hebrew school until he was 11. It was then, in sixth grade, that Jeff joined the basketball team. Since he had to attend practice after school, and his parents felt he had more than enough Jewish education, they allowed him to quit Hebrew school.

Jeff's father, Mort, is a successful attorney and an avid sports fan who works out at the JCC. Jeff's parents hoped their son would excel in athletics, attend an Ivy League school, have a distinguished career and raise a nice family. For the most part, Jeff followed the plan. It was at Yale that Jeff met Bonnie, his future wife.

Bonnie was active at the Hillel House on the Yale campus and came from a family with a strong Jewish identity. Her father was a board member of the local Jewish Federation and had once been the president of their Reform temple. Her mother was active in the Sisterhood. Bonnie's father was converted by the temple rabbi a year after he and his wife were married. Everyone in Bonnie's family held their rabbi in the highest regard. She was not only a scholar, but someone who was deeply devoted to her congregants. Bonnie was a well educated, proud, and active Jew — perhaps even a future communal leader.

Today, Jeff and Bonnie live in a beautiful home in the Cleveland suburb of Wandering Hills. They have two children, Adam, who is 14, and Sarah who is 12.

The public school they attend is about 30 percent Jewish, and of the Jewish kids in the school, about half have one non-Jewish parent. Both children attend Hebrew school, and both are members of the temple youth group. Adam had a bar mitzvah, at which he did a beautiful job reading his haftorah. The theme of his party was football heroes. Sarah is looking forward to her bat mitzvah when she turns 13, and already knows her haftorah by heart. The theme of her bat mitzvah party will be Harry Potter.

Without a doubt, Jeff and Bonnie's parents have all the *nachas* Jewish parents and grandparents could hope for. They are thrilled with what they see. But what do you see? What are the chances that Jeff and Bonnie will keep Shabbos — even once? What are the chances that they will ever be invited to a *frum* home for a Shabbos meal — even once? What are the chances that they will ever keep *taharas hamishpachah*, or fast on Tishah B'Av? What are the chances their children will marry Jews? The chances are approximately zero — unless someone shows Jeff and Bonnie, and the thousands of families like them, what they are missing.

Today in America, we are staring into a Mitzrayim-like *galus*. It will eventually culminate in a magnificent *Geulah*, but as the situation now stands, only a tiny fraction of American Jewry will be part of it.

The Difference This Time

There is, however, another possibility. We have everything we need to win this war — to literally transform the face of the Jewish people. The only reason it is not happening right now, at this moment in history, is because our strategy is wrong. As long as we concentrate exclusively on deploying more *kiruv* professionals and developing better programs, we will never do more than save a few passengers on the sinking ship. We need the overwhelming majority of Torah-observant Jews to get involved and make the connection to the tens of thousands, maybe the hundreds of thousands or millions of Jews that could be saved, if only someone would try to reach them.

Consider the impact this could have. For example, the Aish HaTorah Discovery program now identifies about 100 people a week who want to learn more or are open to experiencing a Shabbos. Aish has the manpower to turn them on, but not anywhere enough to work with them individually and move them forward. They are ready, but we are not. That is where a mass of lay volunteers could make all the difference. One hundred people a week, from one *kiruv* program alone, are already primed for change; they only need the involvement of caring fellow Jews to transform that potential into real spiritual growth.

Like Yaakov, we have Hashem's promise that one day He will redeem the family of Israel. Will there just be bits and pieces of the family left, or will it be all of us? With *galus Mitzrayim* as the template for our *galus*, the portents for our future are clear for us to see. Now, as then, the advent of the *Geulah* is entirely in Hashem's hands. But the question of who and how many will be left to experience it, that is very much in our hands.

We can throw our hands up in despair, we can clasp them behind our backs and refuse to act, or we can open them, reach out with them and help bring our lost brothers and sisters home.

Now You Know:

- The *galus* and *geulah* from Mitzrayim teach us the nature of our current *galus* and ultimate *Geulah*.
- Although Hashem promised Yaakov that his children would emerge from Mitzrayim, only 20 percent were saved. The rest had assimilated and died during the plague of darkness.
- Hashem kept his promise of *geulah*; the number of people who were lost was determined by the Jews' freely made choice to assimilate.
- If the *Geulah* were to happen today, the vast majority of Jews would not be included because of assimilation.
- Only a mass movement of grassroots *kiruv*, undertaken by, at minimum, tens of thousands of religious Jews, is a powerful enough force to reach the millions of Jews who stand to be lost.
- Every *frum* Jew has the ability to reach out, in a simple, friendly way, to unaffiliated Jews.

Chapter 2
IS KIRUV FOR YOU?

If you are reading this book, *kiruv* is on your mind and in your heart. But is it in your life? If not, perhaps you are not sure how to begin. Or perhaps you feel it's too daunting and difficult. People have many misgivings about their ability to open the world of *Yiddishkeit* to a fellow Jew. They don't see themselves as the type of person who can inspire others or change another person's life. But these are misgivings that evaporate as soon as you take the plunge. And, as we said before, if you are ultimately still uncomfortable doing *kiruv 1*yourself, there are many ways you can help others to do it and thereby share in the mitzvah.

In this chapter, we will begin by addressing the most common reasons people shy away from *kiruv*. They may be the thoughts you are thinking right now. But as you will see, the problems are usually quite surmountable, and the benefits (which we will discuss

---

Adapted from conversations with Alan Proctor, lay *kiruv* activist.

later in the chapter) of opening another Jew's eyes to Torah overshadow the problems so completely that, once you've done a little *kiruv*, you will wonder how you ever stayed away.

The 10 Most Common Reasons People Don't Do *Kiruv*

1. I'm afraid I won't know the answers to the questions I'll be asked.

Experienced *kiruv* professionals have found that most people do not ask deep, philosophical questions. The majority of American Jews are non-observant not because of profound questions and doubts, but simply because they have never been exposed to authentic *Yiddishkeit*. Their questions usually revolve around day-to-day practices and fundamental beliefs rather than difficult concepts. If you encounter a question you cannot answer, admit it without hesitation, even if the question is something simple that you feel you ought to know. You can say, "I never really thought about the reason for that. Let me find out for you." This answer indicates your honesty, and also illustrates that people can and do adhere to Jewish practices even when they don't know all the reasons.

If you run into a difficult question, ask your Rabbi, or call or e-mail any of the *kiruv* resources in the appendix of this book. You need not fear questions, because every one of them has an answer and it is readily available to you.

2. I don't have anything special to offer. I'm not sufficiently knowledgeable and my home and Shabbos table are not very inspiring.

It may be that when you compare yourself to others in your community, you see yourself as lacking. But even with the most basic yeshiva education, you have a treasure-trove to offer an unaffiliated Jew. Can you read Hebrew, follow a siddur, name the *yamim tovim*, read and understand an ArtScroll *Chumash*? Congratulations! You know more than 80 percent of the Jews in America today.

If you don't feel people would benefit by being at your Shabbos table, choose a different mitzvah to share. Learn a little *Chumash* with somebody each week. Sit next to a beginner in shul. Volunteer at a local *kiruv* organization. Offer to help run a *kiruv* Shabbos in your shul. Focus on your strengths so that you can enjoy and excel in your *kiruv* activities.

3. I have no time. It's too big a commitment.

Many *gedolim* have commented that in our generation, frenzied activity is the *yetzer hara*'s most effective tool. The Internet, e-mail, cell phones and so forth were all billed as time-saving devices, with the implied benefit of leaving us more personal time. But in reality, all of this high-speed technology has forced us to work faster, so that we can produce more in a shorter time. People are now on call 24/7, with no time to rest, recharge and focus on what is really important in their lives. For religious Jews, however, there is Shabbos, "an island in time," which provides even the busiest household with an opportunity to invite guests or spend time learning with someone.

Alternatively, you can try to designate one hour a week for a *kiruv* activity. Maybe you can learn with someone over lunch once a week, or become a mentor for Partners in Torah. Perhaps there is a program in your shul with which you could become involved.

If you are really and truly stretched beyond your limit, get to know a local *kiruv* professional. Keep his phone number or that of his organization in your wallet. That way, when you encounter somebody who has an interest in Judaism, you have a number at hand to pass along. If possible, make the call on the spot and make the introduction yourself, so that you can be sure the connection is made. There is always something you can do.

And for the person who still just doesn't want to or is truly unable to get involved, you can at least donate money to a *kiruv* organization!

4. My family is my first priority.

There is no contradiction between tending to your

family and doing *kiruv*. In fact, *kiruv* might easily become one of your family's most valuable activities. Whether you bring Shabbos guests into your home, or participate as a family in a local program, your children will enjoy the experience and benefit from it as well. You will be demonstrating for your children that *ahavas Yisrael* is real and important to you.

If you are worried that your children will find contact with non-religious Jews to be confusing, prepare them. Explain that not everybody has had the opportunities they have had to learn Torah and do mitzvos. Just as we share our money with those who are in need, we share our spiritual wealth as well.

But if you are still concerned, discuss it with your *Rav*. There are personal situations where one should not expose his family to outside influences. Yours may be one.

5. I can't make anybody *frum*.

No one can. The goal is to develop genuinely caring relationships with fellow Jews, which will give them an opportunity to become exposed to a Torah home and lifestyle. The impact of this exposure develops over time, in the normal course of your lives, as they see first-hand the rhythms of Jewish life — Shabbos, *yamim tovim*, family *simchahs*, even the way in which you handle challenges. It is that personal connection which is the most potent force of all.

6. I won't be able to find anything in common with someone who is not *frum*.

You may have more in common than you realize. For instance, if you encounter a *kiruv* prospect in your workplace, you will have your business or professional field in common. With someone else, you might share an interest in sports or a particular hobby. Initially, your relationship will not be based on *Yiddishkeit*. The only role religion plays at first is that the person has expressed some interest in being exposed to it.

It is not necessary to solicit strangers on the street to teach them about Judaism. The most effective and natural way to do *kiruv* is to foster connections with people you meet in the course of your life who ask you a question or express an interest in something Jewish. If this person is somebody you like or feel you could like, get to know him better. People will give you the opening; all you have to do is become aware of it and learn how to act on it.

7. *Kiruv* organizations are doing the job. Why do they need me?

With over 5,000,000 unaffiliated Jews, and under 5,000 full-time *kiruv* professionals in the United States, *kiruv* organizations are vastly outnumbered. Without widespread involvement across *Klal Yisrael*, the job will not get done. During the past few decades, the heyday of the *kiruv* movement, tens of thousands of Jews have come back to *Yiddishkeit*. But during that same time period, we lost over a million Jews through assimilation. Everyone is needed.

8. I do other mitzvos. *Kiruv* isn't my thing.

Kiruv is not just a nice thing to do. It's a mitzvah, an obligation. Just as no Jew would ever say to himself, "Davening isn't my thing, I don't have the time," or "Pesach isn't my thing, it's too much trouble," one cannot just dismiss *kiruv*. The responsibility one Jew has for another is not optional. But even if *kiruv* seems out of character for you, you will find that, like every other mitzvah, Hashem has given you the assets you need to fulfill your obligation. Once you get started, you will quickly discover the many strengths you bring to the table, and the many benefits you gain by putting in your effort.

9. It's not my business to tell others how to live. If they don't want to keep the Torah, that's their choice.

Imagine you saw somebody about to jump off a building. You would never just walk away and say to yourself, "To each his own. Let him jump if he wants." You would do everything you could to convince him not to jump. If you didn't know what to say, you would try to keep a conversation going with him while calling for help.

Our fellow Jews are not jumping off buildings; they are falling off, unwittingly, because they are walking around blindfolded. In most cases, all you have to do is show them what the world looks like without a blindfold. They can see for themselves how much more vivid, meaningful and enjoyable it is. If you can't accomplish that yourself, you can certainly keep a conversation going long enough to introduce them to someone else who may be able to help. Even if they won't remove the blindfold, you can at least help them loosen it a bit and let in a little light.

Most Jews adhere to a secular viewpoint out of ignorance, not by choice. A real choice can only be made if we expose them to authentic Torah Judaism, educate them properly and welcome them into our communities. Once they know enough to make an educated decision and really exercise free choice, a great many of them will choose *Yiddishkeit*.

10. I'll think about it.

Do think about it, but not for too long, because with each passing minute, there are hundreds of thousands of Jews out there dating and marrying non-Jews, being approached by Christian missionaries eager to help them with their problems, joining ashrams, enrolling their children in public schools and looking for meaning in all the wrong places. Every day we spend thinking rather than doing, we lose more people, and their children, and their grandchildren, forever.

As you can see, most of the reasons people shy away from *kiruv* do not reflect the reality experienced by those who become involved; but that is only half the story. The other half is comprised of the tremendous benefits experienced by any person who reaches out to share *Yiddishkeit* with a fellow Jew. There is an unmatched feeling of inspiration and excitement in opening another person's eyes to the Torah's beauty. Inevitably, as the "tour guide" on someone else's spiritual journey, you will notice and appreciate, as never before, the way of life you may otherwise take for granted.

The Top 10 Benefits of Being Involved in *Kiruv*

1. Working with somebody who is learning from the beginning causes you to re-examine your own performance of mitzvos.

Perhaps you have had this common experience: Somebody approaches you with a simple question like "Why do religious men wear a head covering?" You explain that it makes us conscious of G-d's presence at all times. At that moment, you realize that you cannot remember the last time that your *kippah* actually reminded you of G-d's presence. You habitually wear it without thinking, and in doing so, lose so much of the mitzvah's value. But when you become involved with someone to whom the mitzvos are something new, you, too, begin to think about what you are doing. Teaching others puts new life into your *avodas Hashem*.

2. *Kiruv* reignites your connection with Hashem.

Three times a day, every day, we say the same *Shmoneh Esrei*. Every morning we put on our tefillin. Every Shabbos we have three *seudos*. Naturally, we often perform these habitual acts without recognizing that each of them is a vehicle for connecting to Hashem. If this happens to you, your connection is weak. It's as if you are listening to a radio that is not quite tuned to the station. You hear the music, but only through a thick cloud of static. When you do *kiruv*, however, someone else is listening in with you. You are aware and motivated to make sure that the radio is precisely tuned, and both of you benefit from the clear connection.

3. *Kiruv* enhances your appreciation for the Torah community.

If you grew up *frum* and have always lived in a *frum* community, you may have lost sight of what a truly unique and beautiful life we have. In a world in which the family structure is rapidly decaying, we have close-knit families that are devoted to each other. In a world where many people do not know their next-door neighbors, we have communities in which

Is Kiruv for You?

hundreds of people know each other and support each other in times of joy and times of sorrow. In a world in which people are morally adrift, we have *Rabbonim* whose Torah wisdom guides our decisions. Our spiritual relationship with the *Ribbono Shel Olam* gives us strength in times of crisis and encourages us in times of weakness. When you get to know others who are bereft of Torah, you will see and appreciate the absolutely incredible lives we live.

4. By bringing Hashem's lost children home to Him, you earn Divine gratitude.

Imagine you lived in a country ruled by a king. He had one child, a daughter, whom he loved more than anything in the world. One day, the daughter set out to visit a distant city, and she lost her way. The king dispatched his guards to find her, but she could not be found anywhere. The king was desperate, fearing that his daughter was gone for good. He sent word throughout the country that he would give a $10 million reward to the person who found his daughter.

Soon thereafter, you were walking down the street and noticed a young woman walking alone, looking as though she were lost. You took note of her, but just shrugged and walked on. On a signpost on the next block, you spotted the king's announcement offering $10 million to the one who could find his daughter. You recognized from the picture on the poster that the woman you had just seen was the missing princess. Would you simply continue on your way, or would you turn back and try to relocate the princess and bring her back to the king? There is no question that you would run back to find her, rescue her and claim the $10 million. No one would bypass such a vast reward.

But that reward is just a tiny glint of the reward Hashem bestows on those who bring His lost children home. While the king in the allegory has only a finite gift to offer, albeit a grand one, there is no limit to the Divine storehouse of merit in the next world and blessing in this world (*Chovos Halevavos,* Gate of Love of G-d, chapter 6).

One might wonder, if Hashem wants His children back so badly, why doesn't He just redeem them Himself? The answer is that doing so would eliminate the free choice with which He has endowed each of us. He can lay out a path before a person, but He cannot make him walk it. When our paths cross with that of a fellow Jew, we have an opportunity to achieve the ultimate Divine gratitude. We encounter the "lost princess" each and every day; only a fool would shrug and walk on.

5. *Kiruv* builds a constant, ongoing source of merit for *Olam Haba.*

When a person does a mitzvah, he earns merit in *Olam Haba,* which will be there for him when his life in this world is through. But the merit for *kiruv,* like a fabulous, risk-free investment, keeps on compound-

Is Kiruv for You?

ing, over and over again, without limit. That is because by the act of *kiruv*, you are not only performing a mitzvah yourself, but enabling another person to take on a whole life of mitzvos. Every Shabbos he keeps, every word of Torah he learns, every *tefillah* he utters will bring credit to you. The people who are religious because of our influence produce precious spiritual benefits for us with every mitzvah they perform (*Chovos Halevavos*, Gate of Love of G-d, chapter 6). This is true even if you are only one stop on the person's journey, for had you not been there, perhaps he would have turned back, or taken off in a different direction. Then, if this person marries and has children of his own and raises them to a life of Torah, those children's mitzvos also bring you credit. And all of this is the result of helping, or even partially helping, just one person become Torah-observant.

Imagine the impact of helping two people, or three or four, or even more.

HaRav Aharon Volkin, in his *sefer Netzach Aharon*, explains the famous phrase in *Chazal* of *din v'cheshbon* as follows: *Din* is the judgement itself; whether you are judged favorably or negatively for what you have done. *Cheshbon* is what results in the future from your acts, i.e., your mitzvos and *aveiros*, and how they have affected others. Consequently, when you have brought someone closer to Hashem, He continues to track your multi-generational benefits eternally.

We see, therefore, that the benefits of *kiruv* extend even beyond this world. Once we pass into the next world, our time for earning merit by personally performing mitzvos is finished. We are left with the accomplishments of our lifetime, and nothing more. However, Hashem continues to keep the *cheshbon* for us and the ongoing effects of the *kiruv* we did in our lifetimes keeps the merits flowing. Clearly, *kiruv* is one of the most effective means we have to ensure that our portion in the next world will be a beautiful and ever-growing one.

6. *Kiruv* causes you to focus on spiritual issues you may never have contemplated.

When one grows up in a *frum* home, many religious beliefs are inculcated by one's family and community. There is rarely cause to stop and think about why we hold our beliefs; it seems self-evident. But, if challenged, could you defend your beliefs? Can you explain why our beliefs are any better than those of people brought up in different religions, who also feel they know the truth? It is an obligation to know and understand the fundamental concepts of our religion. Being a friend to someone who is choosing *Yiddishkeit*, rather than having being born into it, can bring about an eye-opening exploration of what you believe. If you already have the answers, you are ahead of the game. If you are not sure, this is your opportunity to find out. The answers are readily available once you start asking.

Is Kiruv for You?   23

7. You will have an opportunity to relearn many things you have forgotten.

Many of the basics of Jewish practice and belief were learned long ago as a young child at home or sitting in a classroom. But when you learn with an adult who is just beginning to travel the path of *Yiddishkeit*, the basics must be reviewed again, only this time on an adult level. You will find yourself refreshing your knowledge, retrieving facts and concepts that might have been long forgotten, and delving more deeply, on an adult level, into concepts that you learned as a child. This is a wonderful opportunity to relearn the basics and deepen your understanding.

8. You will have the incomparable feeling and spiritual benefit of saving someone's life.

Imagine you are sitting by a swimming pool reading a newspaper when, suddenly, you hear someone yelling for help. There, in the deep end, you see the person thrashing around, gasping for breath, sinking under the water. You drop your paper, rip off your shoes, jump into the pool fully clothed and swim with all your might to reach the drowning person. Finally, you manage to pull him to the edge and hoist him out of the water. There, you administer first aid and save his life. Can you imagine the exhilaration you would feel when the color returns to his face and he is clearly out of danger? You could not even express the sensation that permeates every fiber of your being. You would still feel a thrill of joy each time you saw him, even decades later, knowing that because of you, he is walking the earth. Because of you, he lived to marry and have children.

Believe it or not, *kiruv* can produce the same effect — not something like that, but exactly that. When you see somebody growing in his relationship with Hashem, beginning to do mitzvos, asking deep questions, slowly synthesizing it all into a new world view, you will feel the same exhilaration as if you had saved him from physical destruction. Years later, when you see this person whom you assisted, and he is part of the community, raising children, doing mitzvos and adding his unique gifts to *Klal Yisrael*, your sense of accomplishment will be indescribable. You will know that this is one of the most important things you have ever done in your life. It is better than knowing you have money in the bank, because this accomplishment will accompany you to the next world.

9. *Kiruv* fulfills four halachic imperatives.

Rav Yitzchak Berkovits explains that according to the Chofetz Chaim (see *Chomas HaDas*, part 1, *Chizuk HaDas, ma'amar 1*), the mitzvah of *kiruv* encompasses four obligations:

a. *Ahavas Hashem*, which includes *kavod Shamayim*, because one's attention to Hashem's spiritually needy children shows love and honor for their Father.

b. *"Kol Yisrael areivim zeh lazeh"* — the responsibility each Jew has for every other Jew.
c. The interpersonal mitzvos of *hashavas aveidah* and *lo sa'amod al dam rei'acha*. The first mitzvah, returning lost objects, is fulfilled by returning the Torah to a Jew to whom it has been lost and by returning Hashem's children to Him. The second mitzvah, that one may not stand by while a fellow Jew is being harmed, informs us that we cannot simply stand by while our neighbors stumble into spiritual oblivion.
d. The Torah curses one who does not uphold and support Torah at a time when the Jewish people need to be strengthened, and it blesses those who do.

10. You can attain all these benefits within the context of your present life and schedule.

Kiruv professionals do not have a monopoly on all these benefits, because some level of *kiruv* can be done by everybody and anybody. As you will see throughout this book, there is a role for each of us. Some people will become inspired and initiate something brand new. Others will connect to an ongoing program. Others will do their part by giving financial support to *kiruv* projects, and others may be able to do nothing more than provide someone with a good book or a phone number. Of course, "according to the difficulty is the reward," but the benefits of doing *kiruv* are there for anyone who becomes involved in any way. The key is to begin. Once you make some kind of effort, you will see that *kiruv* changes your life for the better. You may find that you have more time than you thought.

Chapter 3
PRACTICAL KIRUV

At this point, you understand why it is crucial to become involved in *kiruv* on some level. You are willing to do something, but what? This section will familiarize you with the steps you can take to actually have an impact on someone's life.

The first of these steps is to clarify what we mean by "*kiruv*." Some people mistakenly believe that *kiruv* is accomplished by winning a debate. You will be presented with questions, doubts and outright objections to *Yiddishkeit*, and, according to this view, your job is to shoot down those arguments with good answers. The defeated party would then seem to have no choice but to become religious. After all, he's wrong and you're right. But the fact is that losing an argument rarely, if ever, makes someone change his life to become religious.

In fact, *kiruv* is something very different. It is an

Adapted from a *shiur* by Rabbi Moshe Zeldman, Senior Lecturer, Yeshivas Aish HaTorah.

ongoing interaction with a non-religious Jew, through which he becomes aware of ideas and ideals he has never before considered. His closeness to you and your life is his window on these ideas.

At the end of the first *perek* of *Mesillas Yesharim*, the Ramchal explains that just like iron is drawn to a magnet, every Jew has a deep inner desire to connect to Hashem. Every Jew feels the yearning to grow spiritually. On the other hand, every Jew must deal with the *yetzer hara*, which creates confusion and interferes with the *neshamah's* natural pull toward the Divine. This conflict influences every Jew at his own level.

The mind-set needed to approach *kiruv* is to understand that you are talking to a Jew — a soul that is already, on some level, seeking attachment to Hashem. Your task in doing *kiruv* is to remove the obstacles that stand in the way, because like iron and a magnet, every layer of obstruction weakens the attraction. If you can help a person remove his personal barriers, he will naturally start moving in the right direction.

The inadequacy of the debate model of *kiruv* was proven by trial and error in the early days of *kiruv*. The idea was to bring secular college students to Israel for a three-week touring/learning program. Between tours, the teachers would impart teachings about G-d and Torah, explanations of *Torah Shebe'al Peh* and so forth, in the belief that once the students understood the truth, they would become religious. But they did not. Instead, they became resentful, feeling as if the program was aimed at forcing them to change their lives. By and large, they were happy-go-lucky college kids who saw no great need to give it all up for Torah; they did not want to learn anything that would cast their world view into question.

The failure to reach these students caused organizations to reassess their approach. *Kiruv* had to start by showing people that a religious person can have as much, if not more, enjoyment in life as someone who is not religious. Once they saw that there was joy and excitement in the experience, they would become willing to find out what Torah has to offer. They had to be shown that Shabbos, *kashrus* and the entire structure of a Torah life add immeasurably to one's life rather than ruining it.

Most *baalei teshuvah* will admit that when they first began keeping Shabbos, they found it difficult. But after keeping three or four Shabbasos, they could never imagine turning back. They can no longer even imagine how they survived without Shabbos. This is the message a potential *baal teshuvah* needs to understand — that the transition may be difficult, but the end result is a life that is far more fulfilling.

The secret to overcoming these barriers is to really appreciate the secular Jew's point of view. If his impression is that you want something from him — you want to win, to change him, to score one for your side — he will not be interested in anything you have to say. He will see your proofs and arguments as an assault, not an attempt to help introduce him to a better life. On the other hand, if you are his friend, your words and your life will be meaningful to him. You can tell him things he didn't know, and show him things he has never experienced, and he will be receptive. A *talmid chacham* who is today very successful at *kiruv* tells this story:

> *In my youth, I was a college student, not frum at all, and there was a big Chassidic Rebbe coming to our campus. The Chabad Rabbi suggested that I go see this Rebbe. "He's very worldly. He has studied many things. You should go to him with all your difficult questions." I was a philosophy student, and I did have a long list of issues that bothered me. So I wrote down my 10 biggest questions about life, Judaism and the world in general, and I went to see the Rebbe.*
>
> *I asked him the first question, and he said, "That's a great question! I've never thought of that! I have no idea." I tried the second question, and he said, "I thought of that question once also. I don't have an answer, but it's a very good question." For the third question, he said, "Well, I have a bit of an answer, but I'm not so sure."*
>
> *The questions went on, well past the original 10, but there were no definitive answers. At the end, he said to me, "I see that you are a deep-thinking man. I'm coming back to town in two weeks. Let's sit down for a couple of hours then and really talk it out. I'll bring my books, you bring your books, and we can look up things together."*

> *Slowly, I became a chassid of this Rebbe. If the Rebbe would have answered all my questions, I would have walked away saying, "That's a really smart Rabbi! I'm really impressed." It wouldn't have done anything to me. What made me take Yiddishkeit seriously was the Rebbe's interest in me. He wanted to get to know me. He wanted to help me. That relationship was what created the difference.*

Once you establish a relationship and meaningful interaction with someone, you will discover that there are four fundamental barriers you will have to overcome in order to clear the blockage and let Hashem's magnetic power reach the person's *neshamah*. If you can overcome these four misconceptions, you will be much more successful in fostering real change.

The Four Biggest Misconceptions of Judaism

1. Judaism is a leap of faith.

When you speak to someone about Judaism, you should keep in mind that he believes that all religion is a leap of faith and that being religious has no rational basis. He thinks it is simply a matter of doing what you were raised to do, and since he was not raised this way, he sees no imperative to change. It is extremely important to be able to convey, in some subtle way, that it is eminently more reasonable to believe in G-d's existence and the Torah's Divine origin than not to. If you don't know how to explain this, get guidance or take the person you are talking with to someone else who can.

2. Judaism denies a person enjoyment in this world.

From the secular perspective, a religious Jew works around the clock for Hashem in this world, eschewing all kinds of pleasure, and only sees the fruits of his labors in the World to Come. You have to convey, both through words and by showing the person, the special warmth and joy of Shabbos, *yom tov*, family and so forth, that Torah brings you more enjoyment in this life. Rather than taking the joy out of life, the Torah gives you flawless instructions on how to gain a far deeper level of pleasure.

3. Religious Jews look down on secular Jews.

Unfortunately, this very common impression presents one of the biggest obstacles to *kiruv*. However, if you develop the right frame of mind, you will not only be able to overcome this misconception, but it will ensure that you, yourself, always approach a non-religious Jew with the proper appreciation of who he is.

Imagine the following: You are sitting at a friend's *simchah*, and next to you is a cousin from a non-religious branch of the family. He is a college kid, wearing a lime-green T-shirt under a leather jacket. He has many more earrings than he has ears, including one little silver ring in his eyebrow. His language is atrocious, and he's finding the bar mitzvah boy's speech unbearably funny. When you look at this boy, realize that he didn't choose to become a secular person who speaks crudely and wears earrings. He is this way for one simple reason: that is how he was raised. He is the product of his home, his school, his friends, the TV shows that he watched, the books that he read and the movies that he saw. These are the factors that made him who he is.

Now think of this: You are the way you are for exactly the same reason. If he had grown up where you did, he might be just like you. He might even be far better than you are. And if you had grown up where he did, you would be like him. The fact that Hashem placed you in favorable circumstances does not make you better than he is.

The Talmud in *Sanhedrin* 74a confirms this point of view in its discussion of dying *al kiddush Hashem*. There, one learns that if faced with a choice of killing another Jew or allowing oneself to be killed, a person must allow himself to be killed. The Talmud sees this as a logical conclusion, because "How do you know that your blood is redder than his?" Rashi expounds, "Who knows who is more precious in Hashem's eyes?" As the story below illustrates, this concept has proven powerful in overcoming the impression that non-religious Jews are devalued.

A Rabbi caught a cab in central Jerusalem and settled into his seat. "You know what?" he said to the driver. "I learned something very interesting. The Talmud talks about a case of somebody who puts a gun to your head and says, 'Either you kill this man or I kill you.'

What do you think the halachah is?"

"He has to let himself be killed," says the cab driver. He bears no indication of being religious, but like many Israelis, he is familiar with this concept.

"Right, but do you know why? The Talmud says it's very logical that you cannot kill that guy because in Hashem's eyes, maybe he is more precious than you are."

He gives the cab driver the following scenario:

"Imagine there's a big Rebbe who has thousands of talmidim and tens of thousands of followers. Imagine, somebody puts a gun to that Rebbe's head. He says, 'Rebbe, either you kill this secular Israeli who goes to the beach on Shabbos and eats a ham sandwich on Yom Kippur, or you die.'

"The Rebbe would turn to his talmidim and ask, 'What should I do? Who should die? The secular Israeli or me?' The talmidim unanimously would say, 'Rebbe, you have to die, because we know that in Hashem's eyes, that secular Israeli might be even dearer than you.'

"Why? It is because the secular Israeli perhaps never had a chance to be anything else. This is how his parents raised him. This is what he learned in school.

> Hashem knows what He can expect from him, and Hashem is the only one who can judge his value."
> The cab driver smiled and nodded in approval. As the Rabbi got out of the cab, he knew he had managed to clear at least a little of the path toward this man's neshamah.

It is important to realize that this is not just a strategy; it is the truth. You really do not know if you would look or act any differently if you were in the other person's place.

You might be surprised to know that very often, when you sit next to someone in a cab, on a plane or in a doctor's waiting room, he automatically assumes that you look down on him. Even if you say "good morning," and just sit there learning or reading a book, minding your own business, it is almost certain that the person thinks, *To him, I'm not even a Jew. He's looking down on me because I'm not religious.*

If you do not do something proactive to break this misconception, it will stand. By doing nothing at all, you will automatically reinforce his negative image of religious Jews.

However, you can easily make a difference, simply by talking to the person. If the situation is right, you could give the above *devar Torah* from *Sanhedrin* and explain it as the Rabbi in the cab did. If not, just be friendly. Evince an interest in the person and talk about what's important to him. If he's a cab driver, talk cars and traffic. If he's a teacher, talk education. Show him that you care about what he has to say. You will find that it's not difficult at all to open up a conversation. Most people suffer from a sore lack of close, caring relationships in their lives. Even within marriage, couples are often so self-absorbed and distracted that they barely listen to each other. If you are someone who will listen, you will be welcomed with open arms.

4. Judaism is all or nothing.

People hold the widespread belief that if they become religious, they must make a commitment to take on every mitzvah immediately. Therefore, rather than face the frightening prospect of changing their entire lives overnight, they opt to do nothing at all. The simple antidote to this misconception is to encourage people to make small, gradual changes. Encourage them by letting them know how precious even one mitzvah, performed one time, is in the eyes of Hashem. The important thing is to be moving in the right direction.

If someone is not ready to keep Shabbos, ask them if they can just keep it on Friday night. If they feel they cannot keep it for a whole night, ask them if they can keep it for just two hours — two hours of time around a table with family or relaxing together, without the phone or television. If they are not inclined toward Shabbos at all, let them start with *kashrus*. If not the entire mitzvah, perhaps they can just begin by not eating milk with meat. In other words, you can help them find the one thing they are ready to do *l'shem*

Shamayim, and let them know that it has tremendous value.

> *A very wealthy American came to Israel for a visit. On a friend's suggestion, he enrolled in an outreach learning program for businessmen, where he was scheduled to learn privately for two hours a day, for three days. As one of his teachers entered the room, the man told him, "Rabbi, I'm in shock. I just found out from the last Rabbi I was talking to that according to the Torah, you are not allowed to eat shrimp."*
>
> *The Rabbi confirmed that it was true.*
>
> *"Rabbi, you don't understand," he countered. "I eat shrimp every day of the year. I live near the ocean and from the time I was a little kid, we had a servant who would go to the market every morning and buy us fresh shrimp. I have literally had shrimp just about every single day of my life my whole life. You are going to tell me that I can't eat shrimp?"*
>
> *The Rabbi replied, "Listen, there are another 612 commandments in the Torah. It's not do or die, that just because you eat shrimp you should forget about the rest of the Torah. Every mitzvah counts. Let's forget about shrimp. Can you work on not gossiping about other people? Can you give a little tzedakah? Learn a little Torah? Shrimp is not the only mitzvah."*
>
> *"I hear what you're saying," he said. "But I'll never become religious because I can't see my life without shrimp."*
>
> *"Do you think you could go one day a week without*

shrimp?" the Rabbi asked. "Do you think that you could try, in honor of Shabbos, not to have shrimp?"

The man agreed to try. He went back to his oceanfront home in America, and a few weeks later, he called the Rabbi to tell him that he had utterly failed. Shabbos morning came and he was chafing miserably against the restriction he had accepted. Finally he relented and had his shrimp.

The Rabbi didn't despair. "How about once a month? Once a month, on the first of the Jewish month, you won't eat shrimp. I'll tell you when it is in advance."

He said he would try it, and he did. In fact, he succeeded three months in a row. At that point, the Rabbi suggested upping the ante to once a week.

"I want to tell you something," the Rabbi added. "For that day that you don't eat shrimp, you should realize that in G-d's eyes, you have a much greater reward for keeping kosher than I do, and I keep strictly kosher. You know why? Because the Mishnah says, 'According to the difficulty is the reward.'

It all goes according to the effort. Do you know how easy it is for me to keep kosher? Do you know how hard it would be for me to eat non-kosher? For you, just not to eat shrimp is such an avodah, a service to G-d, it's such a strain that in G-d's eyes you are doing a bigger mitzvah than I am."

He progressed to once a week, then twice a week, and then to three times a week without shrimp. When the Rabbi last spoke to this man, he was eating shrimp *once a month. For him, this was an unbelievable achievement.*

Every step is significant, even little ones. Every effort to do a mitzvah counts. It's not all or nothing.

Now You Know:

- *Kiruv* is primarily about developing a relationship, especially with someone you see regularly in your life.
- The *neshamah* of every Jew is naturally attracted to Hashem. The job of *kiruv* is to help remove the obstacles that thwart the *neshamah*.
- Influencing someone depends on showing care and interest in what is important to him.
- Within the relationship, you must try to break down the four major misconceptions people have about Judaism.
- Sometimes, all you can accomplish is to impart a warmer, more comfortable feeling toward religious Jews.

Chapter 4
DEVELOPING RELATIONSHIPS

Every interaction you have is a *kiruv* opportunity, because your actions and how you treat others can cause a *kiddush Hashem* or, conversely, *chas v'shalom*, a *chillul Hashem*. Therefore, every time you speak with someone you must be conscious of the impact you could have on them. Sometimes a non-*frum* person, even a stranger, will approach you with a question. Answer them respectfully or, if you don't know the answer, offer to call them with it after you have inquired. This may lead to a future relationship where you can share more Torah. But sometimes our job is to plant seeds even if we are not the ones who will have the chance to cultivate them. Ultimately, we

....

Based on a *shiur* by Rabbi Mordecai Rottman, MA, Director of Kol Banayich, an in-reach organization which creates alternative learning programs for at-risk teens as well as providing counseling services, parenting workshops and lecturing.

do not know who or what will influence someone. It is all *siyata d'Shmaya*. Our role is to make the most of each opportunity as it presents itself — even if it is a one-time conversation.

Understand, therefore, that the first step in *kiruv* is intellectually and emotionally extending the concept of Jewish brotherhood to all Jews. Once this bridge is crossed, it will be natural for you to develop a relationship with your non-*frum* brother. It is within the context of this relationship that he can benefit from the knowledge of Torah that you have acquired over the years.

In essence, a Torah-sharing relationship should be and often is a natural part of our relationships with all our brothers, *frum* as well as non-*frum*.

For instance, when you meet a *frum* friend on the bus, you exchange *divrei Torah* on the *parsha*. He tells you about a problem he has with one of his children and you respond with a *vort* of *chizuk* you heard from your rebbe. He smiles gratefully and thanks you as he gets off the bus. In this case, the *devar Torah* might not have seemed outwardly to be a "*kiruv*" *devar Torah*, but in essence it was, because your words have helped your friend overcome obstacles and grow closer to Hashem. That is the real definition of *kiruv*, and it is a life-long mission.

However, you also know that you would not have been able to convey this *devar Torah* in a way that he would appreciate and accept unless your relationship was genuine and personal. Indeed, creating genuine friendships with our Jewish brothers — friendships that enable us to help and encourage one another — is undoubtedly fundamental to our very existence as Jews.

Kiruv rechokim means extending this warm, beautiful part of Judaism to all of our brothers. It means creating genuine, meaningful relationships with others, even when it appears as if we do not have much in common with them. In doing this, you enable a thirsty soul to benefit from the wellsprings of Judaism upon which you have been raised, and to connect with the heritage that has been lost to him.

This is the essential meaning of Hillel's teaching with regard to emulating Aharon Hakohen: "Love people and bring them closer to Torah." Coming closer to Torah is a natural product of a meaningful relationship with the right person.

"But we do not have too much in common," you might object.

You are more alike than you think. Perhaps you both have jobs, spouses and children. At the very least, you belong to the same nation and share a common land. You might even have some hobbies or interests in common. After all, we share the same world. If we look for common ground with others, we are likely to find more than we imagined there would be.

For those who are interested in building new relationships, perhaps this moment, when we stand at a daunting crossroads in Jewish history, is the right time for it.

So take your time getting to know your fellow Jew,

Developing Relationships

share your commonalities and allow time for the Torah you have inculcated within yourself to avail itself to your newly found friend.

In the course of getting to know a person, you should also pay attention to what they are seeking from Judaism and in life. They may already be aware of some lack, some unanswered question that you will be able to address much sooner than you thought possible.

The biggest mistake you can make in this area is to have a one-size-fits-all approach. The psychologist Abraham Maslow once commented, in reference to his fellow therapists, "When all you have is a hammer, every problem is a nail." It is up to you to try to discover what the real need is, and to approach it with an appropriate tool, rather than whatever you happen to have on hand. Is the person looking for a better quality of relationship? Answers to "big questions" about life and death? A sense of community? One can never assume to know, as the story below illustrates:

> *A lawyer once came to learn at a yeshiva. The Rabbi who met with him expected that he would have to argue and offer incontrovertible proofs in order to satisfy the lawyer's sharp legal mind.*
>
> *But when the two began talking, the lawyer described his first Shabbos experience, which had affected him deeply. The meal was at the home of a young baal teshuvah couple. On Friday night, before the meal began, the husband explained that he was*

> about to sing a song to his wife — *Eishes Chayil* — and he asked that the guest not look at his wife while he was singing, implying that it was a very personal moment for the two of them.
>
> "Rabbi, I want to have a relationship like that," the lawyer nearly pleaded. "That's what I want. That kind of relationship, that's what I want."
>
> The Rabbi realized that his reams of explanations were useless, at least for that point in time. This tough-minded lawyer wanted to talk relationships. What he was looking for in Torah was a way to establish a life based on something healthy, loving and respectful. For him, the Torah's view of marriage was the place to begin the journey.

Ideally, when you discover what a person is seeking, you can show him where to find it in the Torah itself. Indeed, his very own thirst for knowledge is the most powerful motivating factor in his excursion into the world of Torah. The more Torah you know, the more tools you have on hand to show the person that the Torah is relevant to his life. If you do not know where to find a certain concept, ask a Rabbi for advice on what to learn. Torah is very powerful. When you are able to address the person's needs with Torah, when you are talking Torah, you are helping the person assimilate it into his very existence in the most personal way.

The purpose here is to find the opening in the person's life, the missing puzzle piece into which some aspect of Torah will neatly fit. However, just because

Developing Relationships

Torah answers one question — even a big question — that does not mean that the person will instantly accept another 612 mitzvos. You will still come to a point, in most cases, where you or somebody else will need to prove that Torah is logical and true.

On the other hand, sometimes even one mitzvah can convince a person of the authenticity of Torah. Another story demonstrates this dynamic:

> *An engineer from New York came to learn in Yerushalayim. He sat down in the beis midrash with a Rabbi to discuss the authenticity of the Torah. The Rav assumed that as an engineer, the man would respond best to logic. However, in the course of several hours of learning and conversing with the man, the Rav felt his message was not eliciting much response.*
>
> *Suddenly, the engineer interjected, "Rabbi, I'll tell you what does it for me. I'll tell you what convinces me that Torah is true. The laws of lashon hara. They are so sensitive, so caring and so understanding. Only G-d could have written laws like that."*
>
> *The Rav realized that, although the man may have been an analytical type of person, he was also a very sensitive human being who felt that social rules accepted by secular society were simply lacking. They violated his inherent sense of right and wrong.*

You might wonder why one mitzvah was enough to convince this highly logical man that the entire Torah is true and G-d-given. An analogy can help to explain: Imagine a person has a computer that is missing an essential piece. He goes from store to store looking for the part, but nothing he tries gets the computer going again. Finally, he finds a store that is stocked with heaps of random computer parts. The owner tells him, "Take your time and see if you can find what you need." He spends hours trying one piece after another until at last he installs a piece, flicks on the switch and all systems are "go." It is apparent to him that this part was made by the manufacturer of his computer.

That is the realization some people come to when they find a mitzvah that puts their life into sync: "This must have been manufactured by the One who knows what makes me tick, the One who created me."

The story of the engineer demonstrates that you must talk to people not only to understand what they're seeking, but also because it is the only way to find out what aspect of Torah might affect them most profoundly. The place to start is with the person himself — the answers he is seeking, not the ones you feel inclined to impart.

Obviously, the stage of imparting information regarding Judaism is dependent on having a relationship with someone who is seeking something from Judaism or, at least, something more from life. However, you might discover that this is not the case. If the person is not interested in learning at this point in their lives, do not pursue it. You cannot argue someone into becoming religious.

Developing Relationships

There is a famous adage, "A man convinced against his will is of the same opinion still." This means that if the person is not interested in Judaism, it won't mean anything to him even if you convince him intellectually. He is exercising his G-d-given power of free choice, and there is nothing you can do. There are many people who see the beauty of Torah, the logic and truth of it, but feel it is simply too difficult for them. You cannot win this argument and, indeed, getting into arguments is neither the intention nor the purpose of your relationship. Consequently, although your relationship may be positive in other areas, do not expect any bridges to Judaism to be built in the near future given this situation.

But don't give up! There are plenty of people with whom you will form relationships who will be interested in your ability to help them reconnect to Judaism. Your obligation is to make yourself available. Hashem will see to it that the right person crosses your path. Your job is to be friendly to everyone and keep your eyes open.

> *There was a man who began his learning career at a baal teshuvah yeshiva and is today a respected talmid chacham. He grew up in a densely populated religious neighborhood, and went to college with many religious students. In all that time, nobody ever reached out to him in any way.*
>
> *Eventually, he went to work in an office where a frum man worked. The man suggested that he go to a*

class. He could see no purpose in it. "I'm a good person already," he said. The man told him that, without learning, he could not have any real idea of what the words "good person" meant. "If you can teach me one thing about being a good person that I do not know yet, I will start to learn Torah," the young student replied.

"Okay," the frum person replied rising to the challenge, "it's a deal."

"Did you know," the frum man continued, "that it is not permitted to inquire of a storekeeper about his merchandise if one has no intention to buy?"

The student was flabbergasted. He had never even thought about that before. The sensitivity of the Torah to human feelings intrigued him. The law was so exquisitely attuned to human psychology. "I'm going to learn!" he decided.

Years later, he bemoaned the lack of interest from the neighbors and fellow students among whom he had lived for so many years. He was certain that, had someone reached out to him, he would have become religious years earlier.

There are so many Jews who want to live the right way. They are looking for someone who can give them a context, a reason and a means to begin exploring. They just need a vehicle; they just need you.

Developing Relationships

Now You Know:

- It is essential to build a personal relationship before attempting to introduce a fellow Jew to Torah.
- To enable this relationship to be one which will allow you to offer your friend a meaningful Torah experience, you must take the time to get to know what it is he is searching for.
- All aspects of your relationship must be sincere and without ulterior motives.
- Some people are not seeking anything from Judaism at present, and one should, therefore, not expect every relationship to have meaningful Jewish content.

Chapter 5
EFFECTIVE FIRST STEPS

As we have emphasized, it's all in the relationship. But obviously, for the relationship to become *kiruv*, it has to move forward. Once you have connected to someone who has expressed an interest in Judaism, you have to decide how to turn his interest into real growth. Some people know what their questions are and will ask you. But there are others — the real "child who doesn't know how to ask" of Pesach Haggadah fame — who are so removed from Torah that they cannot even frame a question.

There are many ways to give someone a taste of what Torah has in store for them, thereby sparking their curiosity and interest in learning. We will offer a few of these fundamental *kiruv* tools here.

Shabbos

Rabbi Ephraim Buchwald, founder of the National Jewish Outreach program, says that Shabbos is one of the most potent weapons in a *kiruv* activist's arsenal. He has been known to say that "for the price of a chicken we can save a *neshamah*." Your first step might be as simple as inviting someone for a Shabbos, or even just for a Shabbos meal.

You probably already have guests at your table, but are those guests ever people who are not frum? You may be worried about your ability to answer every question or your children's ability to behave in an exemplary way. But perfection is not necessary. If you don't know the answer to a question, tell your guest that you will find out and get back to him. Just be yourself at the table. Encourage your children to tell you what they learned about the *parsha* in school. Sing *zemiros* and tell a story. Your guests will be enthralled. If they are not religious, they probably rarely sit down together to a festive four-course meal and spend time sharing their lives with each other. You have something they don't, and when they see it, it will make an impression. They will realize what they are missing and hopefully this will open the way for some gradual changes in their lives.

To ensure that the Shabbos experience is not overwhelming for the guests, keep explanations to a bare minimum. Do not feed them unsolicited information. Just tell them as much as they need to know in order to participate and avoid embarrassment. For instance, show them how to wash and let them know that people don't speak between washing and eating the challah. Other than that, let them take the lead by asking the questions they may have. They will learn the most important thing about Shabbos — its unique beauty — if they are allowed to simply enjoy the atmosphere and soak up the spirit.

But it's not just Shabbos. The Jewish calendar abounds with events that make an impression on secular people: the Purim *seudah*, the Pesach Seder, a meal in your sukkah, a *melava malka*, a *siyum*. Any joyous occasion or personal *simchah*, like a wedding or bar mitzvah, will make an impact.

Conversation Pieces

A very simple, unobtrusive way to open the subject of Judaism is by leaving some interesting Jewish item in a conspicuous place. For example, before Rosh Hashana, you might leave a shofar on your desk at work; before Purim, you might bring in a megillah. Just by leaving it there in view of others, you are bound to arouse questions. This will give you an opportunity to plant a seed of interest.

The item you use for this purpose does not have to be rare or costly. A sign from the Chofetz Chaim Heritage Foundation urging people not to speak *lashon hara* could open up a very productive discussion. So could a Jewish book or magazine, or a tape featuring a good, *kiruv*-oriented speaker on a timely topic.

Even without a prop, you can arouse people's curiosity about Judaism and get them thinking. If it's a fast day, mention that you are not eating. The other person is bound to ask for the reason, and you then have an opportunity to offer a little insight on the day and why it's meaningful to you. If you were at Selichos at 5 a.m. that morning, mention it. Offer a peek into the whole wide world of Judaism that so many Jews never even glimpse.

The Right Places

Bookstores and fairs: Jewish bookstores and book fairs are particularly well suited to *kiruv* purposes, first of all because they expose your friend to a wide range of Jewish issues and topics, and secondly, because he just might buy a book and read it. You could even organize a group to sponsor a local, annual Jewish book fair as a *kiruv* tool, including speakers on a variety of topics, who can also use the opportunity to promote their books.

Beginner's minyan: If someone has already shown an interest in going to shul or learning to daven, find out if there is such a minyan in your area. Ideally, you should check it out yourself first to make sure the program is still running and that the davening and explanations are at the right level. Then, go together with your friend if it is at all possible for you. If you send him alone, he may not find the address, he might feel uncomfortable going in or he might just never go at all. And if he doesn't go, he may never try again, so try to fan the sparks of interest while they are still hot.

G-d 101

Discussing belief in G-d is a typical first step people believe they must take when bringing someone closer to Torah. Rabbis caution never to ask people directly if they are believers at the outset. Their answer may well spring from nothing more than ignorance, yet once it is spoken, they will feel a commitment to defend it, and that may be difficult to break.

Rabbi Noach Weinberg, the *Rosh Yeshiva* of Yeshivas Aish HaTorah, explains this dynamic:

"We get Fellowship students, university students from America, who come to tour and study with us for a while in Israel. As an opening question, we used to ask them, 'Do you believe in G-d?'…We don't ask them that question anymore.

"We found that…once they state they don't believe in G-d, they are atheists. Of course there are plenty of proofs we can show them to the contrary. But once they have taken a position, and you go on to win the argument, you lose a customer. They realize that they don't have a leg to stand on, so they get upset and confused. They end up more devastated than convinced. But you can be sure of one thing: they are not coming back.

"Today, we never ask them if they believe in G-d. We ask them, 'Have you ever prayed?' We will have a group of, let's say, a hundred students and…a hundred hands go up. They all prayed… They don't believe in G-d, but they prayed. Then we ask them, 'Did you ever feel that the Almighty answered your prayer?' Four out of five raise their hands.

"At that point, you might think to ask them the following question, but don't: 'How can you tell me that you don't believe in G-d…if you're telling me that G-d answered your prayer?' Do NOT ask this question. If you do, you will confuse them — thoroughly.

"What we have learned to do is to pick five guys who raised their hands, and we say, 'G-d answered your prayer? Wow! There are six billion human beings and the Almighty answered your prayer. You didn't pay Him anything or bribe Him. Why in the world did He answer your prayer? How did you get His attention? Does that mean that He loves you?'

"All hundred kids say, 'Yes.'

"Deep down, they all know G-d is there and that He loves them. What people don't like are the ramifications and responsibilities that such an admission implies, so they don't easily admit it to themselves."

Eventually, you have to bring this issue to a person's attention. It's your responsibility to do so. However, you have to go about it the right way, at the right time, when your words will be considered and pondered rather than rejected.

Opportune Times

Times of trouble: At certain times in people's lives, they may be more open than usual to new ideas. Often, this occurs when someone faces troubles and is searching for meaning in their suffering. The death of a loved one, illness or a financial crisis can force a person to face questions of life's purpose and G-d's existence.

Obviously, such situations must be approached with tremendous sensitivity. You can't go looking for people in trouble and tell them that they shouldn't worry because it's all part of G-d's plan. However, one thing a person can do is become involved in *bikur cholim,* visiting sick Jews in the hospital. If you can bring them some encouragement and comfort, perhaps through carefully selected Jewish reading material, or just through your presence, you may succeed in making Torah very relevant to a deep, immediate need in their lives.

Be aware, however, that difficult times turn some people against G-d, or make them feel that G-d has turned against them. If that is the case, leave the matter alone. Wait for them to ask questions before offering any guidance. It may or may not be the right time to get into the question of why G-d allows good people to suffer. It might be more helpful to offer to spend time looking into it together at a later time.

When they have it all: Perhaps the best time to influence people is when everything is going well. They are happily married, financially secure, socially active, successful in their careers, but suddenly aware that, having achieved their dreams, they have not really found happiness. Such people need to be reached at just the right moment, when that faint shadow of discontent

Effective First Steps

falls upon their rosy picture of life. It is a fleeting shadow that most people are adept at quickly shaking off by pursuing some new diversion.

College students are also at a perfect time in life to seek answers. They have the advantage of being unattached to a career or marriage that would make major life changes more difficult, and they are at a stage in life when everything is in flux. To influence a college student to make intelligent, well-thought-out decisions as he embarks on the voyage of life is to do a great act of *chessed*. In the upcoming chapter on the "Three Unbelievable Programs" (page 70), you will read about a campus initiative that has been one of the most successful in the history of *kiruv*.

First Mitzvos

When someone is ready to actually do a mitzvah, start with one that is easy, enjoyable and will not conflict with his existing lifestyle. Do not let him add anything new until the first mitzvah has become second nature and is not seen as an imposition. This will help build a stable foundation upon which the individual can grow in his relationship with Hashem.

As mentioned in previous chapters, emphasize that Judaism is not all or nothing. Doing just one mitzvah is not hypocritical. Healthy change and growth occur gradually.

Candle lighting: For women, this is often the first mitzvah to consider. It is easy, quick and quite beautiful to behold. Even if immediately after lighting and saying the *bracha* she turns on the television, the candles bring the soft light of Shabbos into the house for at least an hour into the evening. Do not be tempted to push her further — for example, suggesting that she read a Jewish book while the candles are lit. If she wants to do so, she will. Just express your sincere excitement that she is lighting candles to welcome in the Shabbos.

Tzitzis: Since a person can wear tzitzis under his clothes, it is a mitzvah a man can adopt without making a public statement about his religious commitment. But it must be meaningful, so it is important to thoroughly teach the individual about the significance of what he is doing.

Kiddush: Whether in Hebrew or in English, this is a good first mitzvah for a man. It gives him a way to acknowledge Shabbos, as candles do for a woman, even if this is the only Shabbos observance he keeps at first.

Shema: Both men and women can incorporate this mitzvah by simply reciting the first sentence of Shema each day using a Hebrew transliteration and translation, if necessary. The person should understand that in reciting these words, he is acknowledging Hashem's mastery over the universe.

Shabbos: This is a step 2, after the person has come to appreciate the beauty of Shabbos and has experienced it a number of times with you or other families. If he is drawn to the mitzvah but unsure of whether

Effective First Steps

he could keep it at home, you might encourage his success by suggesting he does not keep all 25 hours at first. Rabbi Yitzchak Berkovits advises that you can even suggest keeping Shabbos for just five minutes — something virtually anyone can do. Slowly he can expand the time; on your part, you should suggest ways of making those few minutes of Shabbos meaningful. Point out that if she is lighting candles or he is making Kiddush, they are observing Shabbos during that time. They will feel a tremendous sense of accomplishment and be motivated to do more.

Be creative. There are many ways to introduce *Yiddishkeit* and make it personalized and compelling. By using the expert guidelines presented in this book, you will be able to benefit from decades of experience in the field of *kiruv*.

Now You Know:

- Ways to bring Torah into the relationship include: a Shabbos meal, casually sharing an interesting Jewish item, book or tape, a trip to a Jewish bookstore, fair or beginner's minyan.
- Opportune times to introduce *Yiddishkeit* include challenging times when people are looking for encouragement; good times when people feel that something is missing from their happiness; during college when people are open to change.
- Good first mitzvos include candle lighting for women, wearing tzitzis or reciting Kiddush for

men, reciting the Shema for men and women.
- Do not start your outreach discussions by asking someone if he believes in G-d.
- Avoid pushing people too quickly to add new mitzvos.
- Encourage small steps and emphasize that it's not "all or nothing."
- Once someone has experienced Shabbos a few times and learned about it, encourage him to try keeping it on his own — for five minutes!

Chapter 6
HELPING JEWS FIND G-D IN SHUL

According to many *kiruv* professionals, often, one of the first things a potential *baal teshuvah* notices about an Orthodox shul is the noise. Unfortunately, in many shuls, people are whispering, talking and milling about while *tefillah* is in midstream. It comes as an unwelcome shock to someone whose only exposure to shul has been his local Conservative or Reform temple, because in those institutions, the congregants sit in reverent silence. They may not know how to daven. They may be there to hear the choir or the rabbi's speech or to display their new fall wardrobe. However, they know that the temple is G-d's sanctuary. This sense is all the more acute because in many cases, the temple is the only location in which G-d enters their lives.

Adapted from a *shiur* by Rabbi Menachem Goldberger, the founding *Rav* of Kehillas Tiferes Yisroel of Baltimore, Maryland.

Creating a *kiruv*-friendly environment in a shul is a challenge for other reasons as well. In fact, many *kiruv* professionals observe that the most difficult part of helping someone to become *frum* is getting them involved in a shul. How could that be?

1. The talking shows disrespect and disinterest, which is contrary to everything they are being taught about the beauty and importance of prayer.
2. Too many shuls make no effort to greet newcomers. It is possible that no one will say hello or wish the visitor a "good Shabbos."
3. Newcomers may be unable to follow the davening and find no one offering to help.
4. The attention they do attract tends to be the wrong kind — a *kiruv*-ignorant person approaching to correct them or comment negatively on their clothing, for example, if it does not meet standards of *tznius*.

But it only takes awareness and a little extra effort to turn a shul into the cornerstone of a *baal teshuvah's* spiritual growth. Jews who feel comfortable and welcome in Orthodox shuls when they come to visit — for whatever reason — will come back again and again.

Rabbi Menachem Goldberger sees this as an essential mission for shuls to undertake, for without this awakening, *baalei teshuvah* are literally without a spiritual home. He presents two typical examples of people to whom a shul can and should be a major source of support. The first example is the young man or woman returning from a few years learning in a *baal teshuvah* yeshiva or seminary in Israel. When they return to America, where do they go? In the best case, they may have a *frum* family they can adopt, providing a framework around which they can begin to construct the rest of their lives. But for those who are not so fortunate, life is lonely. Their own families cannot give them what they need, and the traditional yeshiva world is still an enigma, differing in significant ways from the institutions in which they have been learning.

For such people, shul takes the place of family. According to Rabbi Goldberger, "there are things that we can and should be doing for these Jews who have come home. They need more than a *shiur*, and they need more than *tefillah*. They need to feel that they belong here, in this shul, surrounded by a group of people who care about them. They need to feel that when they make a *bris* or a bar mitzvah, there are people who will be a part of their *simchah*, people who are like family. And that has to do with cultivating an atmosphere of community."

Another category of family are future *baalei teshuvah* who live right there in the community. They are working, raising their children and living their lives when something happens to motivate them to seek a closer connection to *Yiddishkeit*. Perhaps they meet somebody *frum* who influences them, or they hear a *shiur* or read a book — whatever drives them, they decide one day to walk into an Orthodox shul. What will happen to them?

It is essential that somebody greet them (provided one is permitted to talk at that moment) and say, "*shalom aleichem*, nice to meet you, let me help you find a seat." To walk into a shul and feel that people are glad you came is a completely different experience than standing at the door alone and unnoticed. One greeting by one person creates the perception that this is a friendly, warm place. The visitor feels that he has been welcomed into the community.

This is especially vital if the family is on the road to becoming religious or has already committed. They need a place where they feel that their new lifestyle is understood and accepted, as inevitably they will experience a loss of connection with some of their old friends. As much as they need *shiurim* and a place to daven, they need a place where they can feel that they belong. They need to meet *frum* families with whom they have something in common — similar careers, circumstances, needs or goals.

There are several ingredients that we can enhance in our shuls to ensure that they draw in, rather than push away, Jews seeking a spiritual home. They are:

- Friendship
- A non-judgmental approach
- A family orientation

Friendship: "Make Yourself at Home"

Many shuls are not friendly places for newcomers. That is not because people are unkind, but simply because they are complacent in their own worlds. The stranger walks into a situation in which most people already know each other. Many have been friends for years — sometimes since childhood. Therefore, unless someone draws them in, they are left alone on the sidelines.

Shuls can help break down these barriers by cultivating a spirit of friendliness and awakening people to their obligation to greet everyone — not just their own circle of friends — with a pleasant demeanor and a smile. A warm welcome makes a vast difference to someone who feels uncertain and uncomfortable and is moving tentatively with his family into untested waters.

For a shul to be consistently warm and welcoming to newcomers, the concept has to be proactively promoted. Congregants have to be reminded that this is the image the shul wants to project and that everyone counts in making it a reality. With an active, committed stance toward creating a warm welcome, a friendly atmosphere will permeate the shul and people will feel it. They will know they have entered a place where they can find support for their spiritual growth and can really soar to new heights.

A Non-judgmental Atmosphere

The first time someone walks into a shul — even someone who has been going to shul all his life — he will usually feel some nervousness about what kind of atmosphere he is entering. Will he feel comfortable or out of place? Will people stare at him or greet him warmly? Obviously, these anxieties are magnified a hundred-fold when a person walks into an Orthodox shul for the first time in his life.

This relates once again to the greeting the newcomer receives. If he feels that people are "sizing him up," his initial discomfort will be reinforced. All he needs to see are some smiling faces and welcoming gestures to break the tension and allow him to feel that this is a community in which he can find his place.

A Family Orientation: Women and Children Welcome

When a shul is trying to define itself as a community in which members are part of each other's lives, it must remember to embrace the entire family. A husband may walk home from Shabbos davening feeling that this is the best experience of his life, but if his wife feels that there is nothing there for her, the *kiruv* job is only half done.

To complete the picture, the woman must also have a sense of belonging. This can be fostered by providing a women's *shiur*, making sure she develops a relationship with the *Rav* and especially the *Rebbetzin*, and also by ensuring that she feels her children have a place in the shul.

Rabbi Goldberger's shul has taken the initiative to

give women an active involvement in the community with approaches such as:

A family shalosh seudos: Unlike most shuls where *shalosh seudos* is the preserve of men only, this one includes a women's section where the women can partake in the food, listen to the singing and *divrei Torah*, and socialize with other women in the community. Children can also come, and the noise they add is graciously tolerated. During the milder weather months, attendance is about 30 women and 50 to 60 men.

Encouraging a relationship with the Rebbetzin: Women who are new to Orthodox Judaism need a woman they can talk to, whose door is always open to them. This is a role filled in Rabbi Goldberger's shul by his wife. Both the *Rav* and *Rebbetzin* make a point of introducing themselves to newcomers and encouraging them to visit or call.

Rabbi Goldberger's aim is to convey to newcomers that the shul is a wholesome place where their entire family can fit in and thrive. He sees friendship, a non-judgmental atmosphere and family as the three components a shul must provide in order to be *kiruv-*friendly.

"It cannot be left to chance," he urges. "The *Rav* and the administration must identify these goals and emphasize them in every aspect of shul services and programming."

Some Practical Advice for Making Your Shul *Kiruv*-Friendly

1. Set up a *kiruv* committee that includes the Rabbi and President to set goals, choose programs and lay out a *kiruv* calendar spanning a full year.
2. Contact Project Inspire, AJOP, the Association of Jewish Outreach Programs and NJOP, the National Jewish Outreach Program, as well as Agudas Yisrael, Orthodox Union and Young Israel for programming ideas. Their websites offer loads of proven ideas for you to try. (See the appendix.)
3. Appoint subcommittees for each program, which will report on their progress and what assistance may be needed at each *kiruv* committee meeting.
4. Include *kiruv* success stories in your shul bulletin.
5. Encourage all members and shul-goers to participate in your programs because they will gain from it, not just because they are helping someone else.
6. Promote conscious friendliness and reaching out as family to all Jews, especially in shul.
7. Use advertising and public relations to promote your shul and especially the programs for those who want a taste of *Yiddishkeit*.

Now You Know:

- Factors that turn newcomers away from shul include: noise during davening, a lack of friendliness toward newcomers, an inability to follow the davening and a lack of people offering to help.
- A proactive effort to make shuls *kiruv*-friendly could transform them into a spiritual home for those coming home from *kiruv* yeshivos in Israel, or local families "testing the water" of Orthodox Judaism.
- To attain this goal, shuls need to cultivate friendliness, a sense of belonging for the entire family, women and children included, and a non-judgmental atmosphere.

Chapter 7
THREE UNBELIEVABLE PROGRAMS YOU CAN JOIN, EMULATE OR SUPPORT

Your Learning Partner Is Waiting!

If you could create a spiritual satellite photo of America, you would see on it thousands of sizzling sparks of Torah streaking back and forth across the country. These sparks would be carried by phone lines that connect Jews in cities and towns all over the country to frum men and women eager to share some of their religious knowledge with fellow Jews. Over the course of time, you would see that many of these sparks ignite into strong flames that send out sparks of their own. That is what you would see, because that is what is happening through Partners in Torah, a project

---

Adapted from a lecture by Rebbetzin Dena Hundert, Ghetto Shul, Montreal, Canada.

of Torah U'Mesorah that pairs people who want to learn with people willing to teach them.

As a model of how lay people can make a meaningful contribution to *kiruv*, Partners in Torah sets the paradigm. All that is required is a willingness to spend a half-hour to an hour a week on the phone with a learning partner. The *frum* partner, referred to by Partners in Torah as a mentor, is matched with someone who seems compatible and who wants to learn the same topic that the mentor wants to teach.

The mentors are not left to fend for themselves in their new role. They are contacted monthly by coordinators who make sure the match is working out well and offer advice to keep things moving forward. Mentors are even provided with a phone card so that their phone study sessions are cost-free. If they have any problems or questions, they can always reach Partners in Torah at its toll-free number, 1-800-STUDY-4-2, or by e-mail at info@partnersintorah.org. To further nurture the *chavrusa* relationships and learning, there are Partners in Torah retreats, where the partners have the opportunity to meet in person.

It might seem intimidating to take on the role of mentor, but Partners in Torah assures every yeshiva- or Bais Yaakov-educated individual that, just by virtue of their upbringing and education, they have assets far beyond what they realize. This is especially true when seen in contrast with the general population of American Jews. Many of those who are seeking mentors are from areas far from major Jewish communities. Some may even be the only Jew in their town. They may not know anything substantive at all about Judaism, such as what Shabbos is, what *kashrus* entails, what tefillin are or how to recite even the most fundamental prayer such as the Shema. Others are more actively engaged as Jews, but are yearning to learn, ask questions and give their Judaism a more meaningful role in their lives.

Those of us who have a religious background are the beneficiaries of a tremendous blessing: Hashem placed us in families and schools that endowed us with a fabulous inheritance. But our lost brothers and sisters are also entitled to that inheritance, and learning by phone offers a simple way to connect to them and share the wealth we've been given.

Partners in Torah's phone *chavrusa* program now has over 11,500 participants. More than 35,000 people have participated in the program since its inception. But it is really just a first step. The ultimate goal is to inspire the partner to move beyond the phone, into the community. Partners in Torah helps find a local class, *kiruv kollel* or other venue where the person can continue on his path of growth. Some families are so inspired that they pack up and move from their spiritually barren communities and relocate to a place where they can live a Jewish life. One man who lived in Alaska relocated his entire family, all of whom were inspired by him, to a Jewish community in the "lower 48."

Coordinators for Partners in Torah are eyewitnesses to the incredible confusion and longing that characterize the American Jewish community. At the same time, they are the awed witnesses to the miraculous transformations that are not only possible, but are happening every day. One coordinator tells of a few of her experiences:

> *I contacted a girl in Sylvania, Ohio, who was referred to me by a kiruv organization. She was 20 years old when she first found out she was Jewish. Her father was a Baptist, and her mother had never mentioned that she was Jewish. It all changed when her grandmother died, leaving a request in her will that the daughter be given a bat mitzvah.*
>
> *Naturally, the girl was confused as to why her grandmother would make such a request, and, of necessity, the truth came out. I called her within a year of that discovery and offered a learning program. I told her it's free and she can learn anything she wants over the phone with someone selected just for her. She couldn't believe that there was anything that was really free. She was so incredulous that someone was going to talk to her about anything she wanted to talk about. She's been learning ever since."*
>
> *Another high school girl I spoke to told me about the "Survival Kit" book by Rabbi Shimon Apisdorf that she had gotten through the kiruv organization that gave me her name. She loved it so much that she brought it to school and shared it with all of her friends.*
>
> *Then she told me that she's very into outreach in*

her school. She is part of USY, which is a Conservative youth movement. She said she would love to learn more and tell her friends about it. So I got her involved with a weekly telephone conversation.

Now she's a senior. Where she goes to school next year can easily influence the rest of her life. She might go to college, but what if we provided her with information about a year of learning in Eretz Yisrael? She could learn a little and change her whole life a lot.

My favorite story is about a family in Lubbock, Texas. In the course of my first conversation with the mother, she told me that she was raised in an extreme ultra-Orthodox community. But as a child she wasn't taught about the meaning of anything she did, and so she drifted away. Fortunately, she married in the faith, but her husband was Reform.

At that point, the woman told me that lately she was feeling a thirst for learning. She remembered that she used to learn midrashim from a text, and she wanted to learn again. It might have all been inspired by the fact that she felt there was a void in her family.

As I signed her up, her husband grabbed the phone. "Wait!" he said. "I want to learn, too. I'm struggling to learn Hebrew right now. I just started making Kiddush, but I don't really know what I'm supposed to be doing. My wife has all this knowledge, but I never grew up with anything, I'm eager to learn. I also have a son here, who is 17. He's been telling us that he wants to be a Reform rabbi, and now we've started taking him seriously. The rabbi of our Reform shul just left and my son is ready to take over — he just doesn't know what to do."

So after I spoke to the husband and got him set up, I spoke to the son and set him up with a phenomenal mentor. Then I found out the couple also has a daughter who was studying at Brandeis. She always thought she knew what being Jewish meant, until she got there and discovered there was a lot more than she knew. I called a friend and got them connected in learning. Now this whole family is learning Torah and developing a relationship with Hakadosh Baruch Hu. G-d willing, the son will be a rabbi one day and, hopefully, it will be for an Orthodox shul. Who knows?

Every day, Partners in Torah finds new people who want to learn, but many more mentors are needed. If you are reading these words and you have a basic Jewish education, this message is meant for you. Seize the opportunity to reach out to a fellow Jew. You can be someone's inspiration!

Now You Know:

- Partners in Torah can pair you with a compatible phone *chavrusa* who wants to learn.
- Learning sessions take only 30 minutes to an hour per week and can be on any topic you feel comfortable teaching.

- Partners in Torah has been the catalyst for many people to begin learning and observing Torah.
- Many more mentors are needed to accommodate the numbers of people who want to learn — a number that grows each day.

Is There a College Near You?

The Collegiate Learning Exchange (CLE) was begun by a group of idealistic laymen who perceived a problem and took upon themselves the responsibility to do something about it. The resulting college outreach program, one of the most successful ever created, is now being replicated on other campuses.

In less than five years from its inception, CLE has been instrumental in inspiring 80 young people to become *shomer Shabbos*. Under CLE's auspices, 165 previously unaffiliated students have learned in Torah programs in Israel. Thirty to 40 students are participating in a weekly CLE-sponsored Partners in Torah program with local community members, and between 50 and 90 students regularly attend its *Shabbatonim*.

If there is a college in your area with Jews on campus, this is a program you should consider initiating.

Adapted from an interview with Dr. Paul Kurlansky, MD.

Three Unbelievable Programs

Campus *kiruv* is not new. It is, however, tragically underemphasized, because college is where:

- 350,000 to 400,000 young Jewish men and women can be found — two-thirds of them concentrated on just 100 campuses.
- Young Jews are at an intellectually and emotionally open stage of life, unfettered by marriages, children or careers that could lock them into an assimilated, or even a gentile, lifestyle.
- Students live outside their parents' homes and are therefore free to adopt a lifestyle different from that of their parents.
- Many Jewish students are cast into an identity crisis due to a steady diet of anti-Semitic messages delivered through radically leftist (and sometimes Saudi-funded) courses.
- Many Jewish young people part ways with their Jewish traditions for good.

Given these factors, campus *kiruv* needs a new injection of life, and at UCLA, Rabbi Moshe and Rebbetzin Bracha Zaret stepped up to the challenge. The program they started, JAM (Jewish Awareness Movement), dispatched young, dynamic *Rabbonim* to the UCLA college campus to create a buzz of excitement about Jewish life and learning. It worked. Suddenly, the pull away from Judaism reversed, and in its place, a powerful magnetic attraction pulled students into

Shabbatonim, learning programs and other positive Jewish experiences.

Rabbi Shmuel Kalos of Ohr Somayach, Miami Beach, Florida, heard about JAM's success and felt an imperative to bring something similar to campuses in South Florida. If it could be done — if Jewish college students could not only be kept from disposing of their heritage, but actually encouraged to embrace it — how could he not try? He discussed his idea with Dr. Paul Kurlansky, and CLE was born.

The decision was made to begin with a pilot program on one campus, and if it worked, to copy it elsewhere. Incredibly, by replicating it on just 100 campuses nationwide, it would reach more than two-thirds of America's Jewish college population.

The first crucial decision was to choose a campus Rabbi. He had to be someone who could see life from the students' perspective, and he had to be sincere. The campus Rabbi would live on campus and be the personal face of Torah Judaism for these students. Therefore, it was essential to choose the right person for the job.

Once the campus Rabbi was chosen, he would work toward these three goals that CLE set:

Goal 1: To be *mekarev* as many Jewish college students as possible. Ideally they would all become Torah observant, but even if many did not, their greater attachment to Torah could still ensure that they would avoid intermarriage and thereby be able to raise Jewish children.

Goal 2: To involve the local community in *kiruv*. This not only greatly assists in achieving Goal 1, but it also elevates the entire community in many ways.

Goal 3: To develop a model that can be exported, with local modifications, to other campuses and other communities. Wherever possible, CLE would look for opportunities for synergy, using all the resources available to accomplish this essential job as quickly and efficiently as possible.

How to Start

Below, CLE has outlined the steps it took to establish its pilot program on the campus of the University of Miami. Adapted to local circumstances, these steps can be used by anyone who has a campus in his area:

1. *Assemble a board:* We found individuals who understood the problem, had a vision of what we could accomplish and could fund the program. Our original board included around eight people in addition to the founders, Rabbi Kalos and Dr. Kurlansky.
2. *Select a campus:* Although Gainesville (University of Florida) has 6,000 on-campus Jewish students, we live in Miami. Therefore, to maximize our ability to manage and be involved in the program, we chose to begin with the University of Miami (UM), even though its Jewish population was only 2,000.

3. *Coordinate with existing programs:* We contacted UM Hillel to find areas of joint benefit. They could provide a building, a name and infrastructure. We offered talent and programming. At that time, the UM Hillel was struggling, and therefore our offer of a free Rabbi was warmly welcomed.

    We also made contact with Ohr Somayach and Aish HaTorah. Neither of these institutions was focused on college *kiruv* at the time. However, when Aish subsequently made a major commitment to campus outreach nationwide, our experience provided useful input for designing its program.

4. *Make connections with the administration:* We sent an e-mail to the President of the university introducing ourselves. She referred us to the Vice Provost of Student Affairs, who happened to be Jewish and was excited about having a rabbi living on campus.

5. *Establish bylaws and non-profit status:* Concurrent with the previous steps, we wrote bylaws and filed for Florida non-profit status. All legal expenses were handled gratis by a board member, and all accounting needs were and are still handled gratis by a community member.

6. *Recruit a Rabbi:* With a financial commitment from each board member, we began recruiting a Rabbi by contacting Ohr Somayach, Ner LeElef, and others. Eventually, we found Rabbi Sam

Bregman. Although he had never run such a program before and had very limited experience, he proved himself to be a true dynamo who built a tremendous program.

7. *Encourage community involvement:* We spoke to the *Rabbonim* of all the shuls, the yeshiva and the local *kollel*, letting them know what CLE was doing. We emphasized that we were not trying to start any kind of alternative shul or yeshiva, but rather were hoping to ultimately bring new people to them and to build the local Jewish community. We did this in the following ways:

    a. Slowly we began to choose homes in the community that we felt were ideal for *kiruv*. Then we organized *Shabbatonim* in which students would stay with local Jewish families and eat at their tables. We would have an *oneg* on Friday night in a private home, at which a community *Rav* would speak. We would also sponsor Shabbos Minchah/*seudah shelishis*/Maariv/Havdalah, at the home of a different family, during which a different *Rav* would speak.

    b. In time, we expanded the community program to include more homes, people and students. Gradually, as the formula was refined, it became more and more successful. The program garnered an excellent reputation, leading to increasing local support and involvement.

c. During the morning, when most college students are in classes, our campus Rabbi learns at the local yeshiva or *kollel*. This way he continues to grow in his own learning and gets to know more people in the community. Over time, many of these people have gotten involved in CLE.

d. In the second year, we started our own Partners in Torah program. Every Wednesday night, local *baalei batim* drive to the campus and learn for an hour or more directly with students on topics of their mutual interest. This past year we added a 15- to 20-minute brief talk at the end of the hour by a community Rabbi.

"Our community involvement is really key," says Dr. Kurlansky, "much more so than most people realize. In my opinion it is what sets our program apart from all others that I know of. Students get to know *baalei batim* who are successful in both their material pursuits and their spiritual lives. It enables students to see that they can have a great and successful career, a great spouse, children, home — everything they want out of life — in the context of a Torah-observant lifestyle. It is a definite deal closer."

8. *Capitalize on off-campus opportunities:* In addition

to CLE's outreach on campus, which includes meeting students, inviting the Jewish ones to coffee, ascertaining whether they are really Jewish, identifying what interests them, inviting them to Shabbos meals with the Rabbi and learning with them, CLE connects students with more intensive programs they can experience during winter, spring and summer breaks. It runs some of its own trips, and also encourages students to attend Heritage Retreats, Ohr Somayach in Monsey or Aish HaTorah in New York. The goal is to pave the way for three or more weeks of learning in Israel during the summer.

Making It Work

To employ a Rabbi and produce well-run programs, funding is an essential component. The Miami CLE program has been gratified by the enthusiastic generosity of many of the people it has approached. For instance, when the board decided that a second Rabbi was needed on the UM campus, they approached one major New York philanthropist for matching funds and, based on the program's successful reputation, received everything they requested. They have also cultivated donors in their own community and sought grants from national organizations. Some expected sources of income have failed, while some unexpected sources have come through.

To remain financially afloat, CLE recommends

starting with a relatively small, manageable program that can be nurtured gradually. To keep overhead low, board members and the Rabbis perform many of the administrative tasks themselves.

As the program has grown, fund-raising has expanded. In its first year, CLE's fund-raising consisted of approaching a few community members who were interested in the cause. In the second year, that small circle was enlarged. In the third year, the first community-wide fund-raiser — a brunch — was held, and in the fourth year CLE organized its first journal dinner.

Despite its efforts to keep expenses low, the one place CLE does not skimp is on salaries for the Rabbis. In order to attract talented people who are willing to bring their families to live on a college campus, the board knows it must offer an attractive salary.

"Fund-raising is a major concern," says Dr. Kurlansky, "but we don't let any of this deter us. We have a mission and we will stay the course. There is no question that, every step of the way, there has been tremendous *Siyata d'Shmaya* and we know that our job is to continue forward. *Hakadosh Baruch Hu* deals with the problems. Every community with a college can and should start a program like CLE, and without a doubt, they will see the same Heavenly assistance we have merited."

Besides money, a program like CLE needs the energy and ideas that will add up to successful programming. The UM experience has proven that a variety of approaches can be successful. The style of the Rabbi largely determines what will work best. Some are most effective when they have the chance to sit down and learn with the students. Others get their best results by befriending the students. As the students get to know the Rabbi and his family, and observe his home life and interactions, they find out first-hand what a Torah life is about. Both of these styles have been extremely successful in reaching students and catalyzing major changes in their lives.

The Bottom Line

CLE's key to success has been its focus on its practical goals while keeping in mind the broader vision: college students finding the beauty of Torah, making decisions that will change their own lives and forever alter the generations to come from them. The logistics and steps needed to get started are just stairs that need to be climbed to get to that ultimate goal, and with the right motivation, there is plenty of energy for the climb.

"If I had ever stopped, in the beginning, to consider what would be necessary to reach this point, I might never have done it," says Dr. Kurlansky. "However, once we got things moving, I viewed and continue to see CLE as a situation in which there really is no choice. Whatever it takes, that's what we'll do. It had to be done and it still has to be done — all over America. When one comprehends the problem and then realizes that the antidote is readily available, in our hands, how can we not act?"

Dr. Kurlansky invites anyone who is interested in helping to expand CLE to more campuses to visit the UM campus and see first-hand what is being accomplished. He can be reached at DoctorWu18@aol.com.

Kiruv by the Book: *Sefer* Distribution Program

One of the key points this book tries to drive home is that even the smallest gesture can have profound repercussions. All we need to do is to vastly multiply the number of those small gestures, and we will begin to see a complete transformation of our world.

The power of the simple gesture is eloquently portrayed by Ricky Turetsky's *sefer* distribution program, which he began on his own in the early 1990s. Ricky is a businessman who lives in Miami Beach, Florida. It was perhaps his natural salesman's optimism that gave him the push to try an idea that was proposed to him by Rabbi Sholom Ber Lipsker from The Shul in Bal Harbour, Florida. The idea, first suggested by the Lubavitcher Rebbe, was to offer a *Chumash* free to any Jew willing to commit to a short daily reading.

Ricky had no idea if anyone would take him up on his offer, but he did have faith in his own powers

---

From an interview with Ricky Turetsky.

of persuasion. On that basis, he purchased a few copies of Aryeh Kaplan's *Living Torah*, which he considered to be the best English translation available at the time. He sat down and worked out a daily two-minute learning program, which he outlined on a chart providing the chapters, verses and page numbers. He decided that he would require only a 30-day commitment from anyone taking a free *Chumash*. Even if they stopped on day 31, they could keep the *Chumash*, as long as they agreed to put it on a shelf in their homes. In this way, Ricky would know that, at the very least, he had planted a *Chumash* in a Jewish home. There was always the hope that someday someone in the household would open it.

In the 15 years since this simple program started, Ricky testifies that "virtually nobody has ever turned me down." In his travels as a salesman, he has had the opportunity to give *Chumashim* to thousands of Jews from every background, including U.S. Congressmen, CEOs of major corporations and presidents of hospitals. He often encounters people who, years after receiving their *Chumash*, tell him that they are still reading two minutes of Torah a day.

Before giving a *Chumash*, Ricky would personally inscribe each one with a wish for the recipient's growth in Torah. After many years, the purchasing, inscribing and shipping became so time-consuming that he combined forces with Partners in Torah. He still raises the money to buy the *Chumashim*, but Partners in Torah sends them out. Instead of a two-minute daily learning commitment, recipients must agree to a one-hour telephone class, once a week for four weeks, with a Partners in Torah mentor on a Jewish topic of their choice. After four weeks, they receive the free *Chumash* — which has been changed to the ArtScroll *Stone Chumash* — along with an offer to continue learning. Ricky sees this as a more powerful way to utilize the *Chumash*, because it provides the follow-up that was missing from his more loosely structured personal program.

Having planted a *Chumash*, along with a short *bracha* for growth in Torah, in thousands of homes, Ricky occasionally has the privilege of seeing what has grown from his planting:

> *One day, Ricky and his wife went to be menachem avel at a friend's home. The husband had passed away and the wife was sitting shivah. The couple had not been religious, and consequently none of those who came to visit appeared to be religious either. But after some time, a religious couple did walk in, just as the Turetskys were about to leave. The woman who was sitting shivah introduced the two couples. "Do you know Ricky Turetsky?" she asked.*
>
> *The man's eyes opened wide in surprise. "Let me tell you something. Many years ago, when I was in med school, I was not religious. A friend told me about a program where somebody gave away a free Chumash if you agreed to read it. I figured, 'Why not?' and called this guy Ricky Turetsky. After reading a little*

Chumash every day, at some point I hooked up with a Rabbi. One thing led to the next, and after a while, I became frum. It all started with the Chumash you gave me!"

Another occasion of being menachem avel was the setting for yet another story. Once again, the family in mourning was not religious, but the Rabbi had gathered the men in attendance for Minchah. Ricky noticed one man who seemed familiar with the davening. When they were finished, Ricky introduced himself to the man and found out that he was a baal teshuvah. His journey had started about 10 years earlier with a weekly Jewish fax to which he subscribed. This newsletter carried an offer of a free Chumash to any subscriber who agreed to the two-minute learning program. This man received his Chumash, did his two minutes of learning a day, and ended up going to learn in a yeshiva for baalei teshuvah. At the point when Ricky met him, he had been shomer Shabbos for about three years. He claimed that if not for the free Chumash, he probably would not have become frum.

Another story — the one Ricky says is his favorite — started with a phone call from a woman in Dallas. Though she had no Jewish background, a friend had told her about the Chumash program, and she was interested. She was sent an inscribed volume of The Living Torah.

Many years later, a new couple moved into the Turetskys' community, and Ricky was asked to help them acclimate. He introduced them to other families, showed them where the kosher stores were and so forth. In the process, the couples became good friends. Just one year later, the new couple decided to make aliyah.

The shul sponsored a going-away kiddush for the couple. In the midst of it, the woman and her husband came to Ricky to tell him something they had discovered.

"You know I usually come to shul with my ArtScroll Chumash," said the woman. "But while we were packing, I came across my old copy of *The Living Torah*. I opened it up to read one pasuk from it, just for old-times' sake. And there I saw it: a note on the front page…from you! That *Living Torah* is what got me started in Yiddishkeit many years ago when I lived in Dallas. Everything I am, everything I have in Judaism, is because you sent me that Chumash." Today, this woman and her husband live in the Old City in Jerusalem.

Torah penetrates the heart. Just give a Jew a *Chumash* — you never know where it will lead.

To refer people to Ricky Turetsky's joint program with Partners in Torah, contact him at ebtur@aol.com or simply reproduce what he did on your own. You can also share in the project by donating money to buy more Chumashim.

Three Unbelievable Programs

Now You Know:

- A simple gift of a *sefer*, coupled with an incentive to read it regularly, can have an immense impact on someone's life.
- It doesn't take a complex program with a large staff to reach out to many Jews.

Chapter 8
99 KIRUV IDEAS

Now that you've had an in-depth look at three successful *kiruv* ideas, you can see for yourself the incredible impact one person can have. But there are dozens of other ways to get involved, and no matter what your particular strengths are, there is something to suit you. The list below serves two purposes: to give you practical ideas you can use, and to illustrate that just about every aspect of our lives presents *kiruv* possibilities.

The first category (1-61) consists of ideas that do not take significant amounts of time, are simple to organize and easy to implement. Ideas in the second category (62-78) require a bit more effort, and the third grouping (79-99) is for those of you who really want to get involved.

Just remember to gear any of these ideas to the person you are approaching. Use simple explanations that people can relate to from their perspective. For instance, don't tell someone that a certain mitzvah will earn him *Olam Haba* if he does not yet believe in an afterlife.

Some of the ideas below will just open doors. Others can help move someone significantly along the path toward *Yiddishkeit*. In either case, there is certainly something — or a few things — here that you can choose and use now. So read on and get started!

Stage I
Shabbos and *Yom Tov* Opportunities

1. Send someone apples and honey for Rosh Hashana with a short note wishing him a sweet year and explaining the custom of eating apples dipped in honey.
2. Blow shofar for people who do not go to shul on Rosh Hashanah.
3. Invite people to eat in your sukkah.
4. Take your *lulav* and *esrog* to a neighbor and help him say the *bracha*.
5. Invite someone to enjoy a *Simchas Beis Hasho'evah*.
6. Invite someone to shul for Simchas Torah and get them dancing.
7. Have a Chanukah candle-lighting ceremony, complete with a *latkes* and *sufganiyot* party and Jewish music.
8. Give someone a menorah and candles or oil with wicks. Include a short note explaining the reason for lighting candles.

9. Bring someone a plate of *latkes* or *sufganiyot* with a note explaining the relevance of oil to Chanukah.
10. Send someone *mishlo'ach manos* with a short note explaining what it is.
11. Invite people to join your Purim *seudah*.
12. Bring someone three *shmurah matzos*, or if there is a matzah bakery in your community, invite him to visit it.
13. Invite people to your Seder.
14. Invite someone to a *tikun leil Shavuos* program. Explain the meaning and purpose of the custom.
15. Periodically place a Jewish book or holiday-related item on your desk at work to encourage questions.
16. Call one or two people on *erev Shabbos* to wish them a "good Shabbos." Give them "Shabbos food for thought" by offering a quick *vort* from the *parsha*.*
17. Invite people to share a Shabbos meal or spend an entire Shabbos with you. Don't overwhelm them with explanations — just relate the basics they need to know to participate in the meal and let them be the ones to raise questions that might occur to them.
18. Make a *melava malka* with a speaker, *zemiros* and food and invite some not-yet-*frum* people, too.

---

* Thank you to Perel Hande for this idea.

Be a Friend

19. Give or recommend this book to as many *frum* people as possible!
20. Invite someone to your home to learn to make challah with you.
21. Grocery shopping can be overwhelming to people who are new to *Yiddishkeit* and *kashrus*. Take someone shopping and show her how to and where to shop for what. Come armed with a sheet displaying pictures or sketches of the major reliable kosher symbols.
22. Invite people to go with you to shul. Introduce them to people with whom they might feel a connection, for instance, people in their professional field. Briefly explain the prayers and procedures as they occur.
23. Greet people in shul who seem to feel out of place. Invite them to sit with you so you can befriend them and guide them through the davening.
24. Invite people to participate in your personal *simchahs*.
25. Be nice to people — consciously! It's not enough to be nice; your warmth only comes across when you also act nice.
26. Show you care about all Jews. For example, when someone is sick, bring food or do an errand for them, even if they say they don't need any assistance.

27. Invite your not-yet-*frum* friend to join an adult sports league or team that includes a lot of *frum* people, if this exists in your community. Introduce them around.
28. Take them to a religious Jewish wedding and offer explanations of the parts of the ceremony and celebration.
29. Take someone with you to a private visit with a *Gadol*.

Get Them Thinking

30. Invite someone to go with you to a class that might interest him.
31. E-mail someone a Jewish article or audio *shiur* on a topic you know would interest them.
32. Give a gift subscription to *Mishpacha Magazine, Jewish Observer* or other appropriate Jewish publication.
33. With the person's permission, sign him up for a Jewish thought-of-the-day or weekly *parsha* sheet e-mail subscription. There are many to choose from, for example, Parsha Perspectives from www.partnersintorah.org (or just e-mail them at parsha@partnersintorah.org) or the Shabbat Shalom Weekly from www.aish.com.
34. Recommend browsing some of the best Jewish websites: ou.org, aish.org, torah.org, simpletoremember.com, etc. (see Appendix for resources).

35. Acquire and hand out short, easy-to-read booklets about Judaism. One place to find these is from Aish, another is the Chofetz Chaim Heritage Foundation, which emphasizes *mitzvos bein adam l'chaveiro*.

36. If their children are currently in public school, get them thinking about a Jewish day school. Recommend one in your area and, if they are receptive, bring them to see it.

37. Teach people the *sheish zechiros*. Each moment they remember any of these concepts, they are performing a mitzvah!

38. Post a "Thank you for not speaking *lashon hara*" sign on your desk (available from the Chofetz Chaim Heritage Foundation). Explain the concept when people ask about it.

39. Learn about and relate some of the complexities of nature and/or the human body, and how this reflects the wisdom of *Hakadosh Baruch Hu*.

40. Teach Jewish business law to a businessman. Here are two laws that are likely to resonate and arouse interest:

    a. It is not permitted to inquire of a salesperson about his merchandise if there is no chance that you are going to buy from him. An example of this would be if you are just doing research or want to try out a product, but you intend to buy it cheaper elsewhere.

b. One may not denigrate competitors or their products. This is routinely done in business today, yet the Torah soundly condemns the practice, permitting one to compete only by promoting the benefits and features of one's own product.

41. If you know someone who recently got engaged, find her a *kallah* teacher. Carefully choose a teacher who is experienced in presenting *taharas hamishpachah* to non-religious people. When presented properly, these laws enhance relationships.

42. Take someone to a well-stocked Jewish bookstore and guide him through the wealth of information there. Place special emphasis on beginner's books. Then let him browse, unimpeded by you.

43. Teach someone who is interested in Israel about the *shemittah* year and the relevant halachos.

Get Them Doing

44. Recommend a "learn about your Jewish heritage" trip to Israel.

45. Put a *tzedakah* box on your desk with a small bowl of change next to it to encourage people to give *tzedakah*. Place a concisely written sign next to it conveying the greatness of *tzedakah* and a brief description of the organization the money will benefit.

46. Encourage someone who is interested in *Yiddishkeit* to choose one mitzvah to do that would have meaning for them. For example, hang a mezuzah, light Shabbos candles, put *tzedakah* in a *pushka* each day. Help them learn the relevant halachos and master this one mitzvah at a pace that they enjoy.

47. Help a Jewish man to put on tefillin. Teach him the meaning and halachos of the mitzvah.

48. Teach someone to say "amen" to your *bracha*. Explain why we say it, what amen means and what it accomplishes.

49. Teach someone to say basic *birkos hanehenin*. Start with one occasion a day; morning coffee is particularly effective because most people truly do appreciate it, and the *bracha* provides a spiritual boost to begin the day.*

50. Most Jews know the first *pasuk* of the Shema. Teach them what it means and encourage them to say it once in the morning and once at night.

51. Give someone a *tzedakah* box from a *frum* organization that performs a service he feels is important. Teach him that Hashem has promised that by giving *tzedakah* we will earn more money, not have less. Encourage him to put some spare change in the *pushka* each day. After two months, call and offer to come over and help

---

* Thank you to Perel Hande for this idea.

him empty it. Deliver or send in a check and get him a receipt.

52. Once a person has been putting *tzedakah* in his *pushka* for three to six months, suggest that he involve his children in giving. Take the family to visit the organization they are helping.
53. Teach or hand out a pocket *asher yatzar* in English with transliteration.
54. Teach or hand out a pocket card of the *sheish mitzvos temidiyos*. Explain to them that every moment they think about one of these principles they are performing a mitzvah!

Build Your Personal Resources

55. Carry with you the name and phone number of a local *kiruv* Rabbi so you can give it out if someone expresses an interest in learning more. If possible, get the number of the person who is interested and have the Rabbi call him or her directly. In either case, follow up with the Rabbi after a couple of days to make sure they made contact.
56. Start, promote and maintain a website of local *kiruv* organizations, classes, resources and tools.
57. Donate money to start, expand or improve existing or new *kiruv* programs in your community.
58. Encourage your friends to join you in organizing a *kiruv* program, either on your own or through your shul.

59. Contribute to, or establish a special fund that is earmarked to buy items for *baalei teshuvah*, such as tefillin, tzitzis, books, learning trips to Israel, etc.

60. Have special *kavanah* when davening the *Amidah* during the *bracha* of *Hashiveinu* for people to do *teshuvah* in general and for people you know in particular.

61. Help people find, learn about and do just one mitzvah. Understand and explain to others that Judaism is not all or nothing — every Jew can find one mitzvah he wants to consciously do without "becoming religious."

Stage II
Learning Together

62. Teach someone the halachos of *shemiras halashon*, which strikes many people as exquisitely sensitive and insightful. There are many user-friendly English books available to use.

63. Learn selected *mussar* texts with someone. Be sure to find out, from your Rabbi or someone experienced in *kiruv*, which *sefer* would be most appropriate for your partner.

64. If you are knowledgeable in the field or willing to explore, learn Chassidus with someone who is interested in a spiritual approach to *Yiddishkeit*.

65. Take someone to a Discovery seminar. (See Appendix.)
66. Escape with them to a luxury weekend at a hotel with the Gateways outreach organization. (See Appendix.)
67. Invite someone to lunch on Rosh Chodesh. Explain the significance of Rosh Chodesh, bringing in the idea of renewal, new commitments and personal growth.
68. For women, especially young women who are trying to find their way in a permissive society, share *hilchos tznius*. Some of the best books in this area, which are short, clear, practical and aimed at today's young woman, are by Gila Manolson. This concept is a wonderful and often welcome eye-opener for the young woman who finds her personal dignity constantly under assault.
69. Encourage non-religious, but traditionally minded parents to send their children to a religious summer camp — especially if their children can go with yours. Be sure to explain to your children the importance of helping them through unfamiliar religious issues or activities and alert the camp to this special opportunity. Of course, care must be taken to match the children with the right camp. However, do not push children who know nothing and have no interest, as it will, in all probability, backfire.

70. Volunteer for a *kiruv* organization.

Programs You Can Start

71. Sponsor or coordinate a Discovery seminar in your shul.
72. Working with your shul or local *kiruv* organization, offer and advertise free High Holiday services that feature explanations of the prayers.
73. Distribute Shabbos candlesticks and candles for women to light. Be sure to include instructions, the *bracha* in Hebrew and English, along with a transliteration, and a calendar of local candle-lighting times.
74. Promote the mitzvah of mezuzah, which is perhaps the easiest mitzvah there is. Find a source for kosher, reasonably priced mezuzos and cases, and offer to put them up with people. Let them say the *bracha* with you and affix the mezuzah to their doors. Tell them that every second it hangs on their doorpost, they are performing a mitzvah.
75. Run a program at your shul, for example, "Turn Friday Night into Shabbos" (see National Jewish Outreach Program in the Appendix).
76. Find a Jewish beginner's book that you think is outstanding and distribute it to Jews whom you meet, on the condition that they agree to read it. For example, before each major Jewish holiday,

consider giving out the *Survivor's Guide* for that holiday by Rabbi Shimon Apisdorf.

77. Recruit *frum* mentors for Partners in Torah.
78. Become a local resource and promoter for post-high-school learning/touring programs in Israel.

Stage III
Make Your Mark

79. f the person you are working with is interested in the Jewish approach to business issues, especially if he is an entrepreneur, learn the sixth chapter of *Baba Kama* with him.
80. Start a kosher cooking class.
81. Write, arrange for or finance a *kiruv*-oriented column in your local Jewish newspaper. A *kiruv* organization would be very happy to help with this.
82. Start a Shabbos hospitality program in your community.
83. Become your shul's Shabbos morning "greeter," who stays near the door to invite newcomers in, find them a seat and pair them with a regular.
84. Start a local Jewish adult education program or work to expand one that exists in your community.
85. Start your own or finance a *kiruv* podcast.
86. If you work in advertising, PR or marketing, ask

your firm to take on a *kiruv* organization as a pro bono client to help it more effectively spread its message.

87. Organize a Jewish film festival in a local theater. Sell or offer booths in the hallways of the theater to Jewish educational and *kiruv* organizations to reach out to attendees. In the program, include articles and ads encouraging people to enhance their Jewish life by taking advantage of what these organizations have to offer.

88. Get involved with your local Jewish Federation so you can meet more non-*frum* people who are leaders in their communities. Let them see that you are normal and concerned about the greater Jewish community, just as they are.

89. Sponsor a *kiruv* professional to offer a local weekly or daily radio show.

90. Start or help build an existing Shabbos beginner's service with your shul and NJOP (see Appendix).

91. Start a Jewish book reading club with monthly meetings to discuss books of general Jewish content. Be sure to invite people of all backgrounds so the discussions will be interesting.

92. Sponsor a monthly or weekly speaker in your home. Invite people of all backgrounds.

93. Sponsor or coordinate a citywide Jewish book fair. Do extensive marketing to the non-religious

Jewish community. Spice it up with speakers, especially authors who want to promote their books.

94. Set up a lending library of Jewish books and tapes for beginners. Let others know you have materials available so that they can suggest it to people they know who are interested in learning.
95. Be a *chavrusa*.
96. Teach a class.
97. Start a *kiruv chaburah*, a group of like-minded religious friends with whom you can brainstorm and develop projects.
98. Start a *bikur cholim* group to visit Jewish patients at your local hospital. Leave behind some Jewish reading material.
99. Become your shul's *kiruv* coordinator and get other people involved doing something positive for *kiruv* (see the next chapter about Project Inspire).

Chapter 9
PROJECT INSPIRE

As this book was being written, a new organization was founded by Aish HaTorah to encourage knowledgeable Jews to reach out to their non-religious brethren. It is called Project Inspire. Project Inspire has already produced two video presentations, "Inspired" and "Inspired Too," which are sounding the clarion call to the frum community to get involved in *kiruv*. The presentations show how easy *kiruv* can be and what amazing results can be achieved over time.

When the founders of Project Inspire heard about this book, they were very excited, because this book picks up where "Inspired Too" leaves off. It provides a practical way for viewers to follow through on the inspiration they invariably feel as they learn about their fellow Jews' courageous spiritual journeys.

Project Inspire aims to rally the 500,000 members of the *frum* community to do their part in reaching out to the rest of the American Jewish population. As mentioned, its first step was to produce video presentations that offer a fascinating glimpse into the lives of Jews who have become *kiruv* "success stories." Whether they are today sitting in Jerusalem learning and teaching Torah, or sitting in a Wall Street law office living the life of a *frum* professional, the people interviewed in these presentations candidly discuss where they came from and what catalyzed their change. Each expresses his boundless appreciation for the opportunity to live a Torah life. The message to the audience is that any one of them can help spark this transformation in a fellow Jew.

That is the "Inspire" part of Project Inspire, aimed at awakening the *frum* world to their power to reach out. The rest of the program — its nuts and bolts — consists of an infrastructure and an opportunity through which people can easily act on their inspiration. It is designed to overcome some of the common reasons people shy away from *kiruv*.

Within Project Inspire's structure, there are three levels of involvement: individual, shul and community.

For Individuals

Give a card or gift: Because people are often at a loss as to how to open a *kiruv*-oriented interaction with another person — even a colleague, relative or neighbor they know well — Project Inspire offers friendly, educational and attractive *yom tov* gift cards that a person can give or attach to a *yom tov*–appropriate gift. So far, it has provided a *mishlo'ach manos* card, a humorous and informative Pesach kit, a Chanukah card and a Rosh Hashana card. It also offers gifts at a low cost.

The information in the cards is designed to open discussion. This makes it easier to begin or continue to build a relationship.

"Care and Share": Someone who has only 10 minutes a week to invest in *kiruv* can still make an impact. All that is asked of participants is that they spend those ten minutes developing a friendship with a fellow Jew, even if at first the topics of conversation seem completely unrelated to Torah. Project Inspire offers "*kiruv* coaches" who will call with a reminder, encouragement and advice on how to reach out.

Shuls and Communities

If individual efforts can accomplish so much, an organizational umbrella that unifies those individual efforts can surely accomplish much more — a working, ongoing movement that will keep rolling forward until every Jew who can be reached is reached. Therefore, one of the highest-impact contributions an individual can make is to organize his shul or community by becoming a local contact person or *kiruv* coordinator. Project Inspire provides the tools for anyone willing to do this.

To further support your efforts, Project Inspire's strategic plan for each community structure involves setting up branches consisting of a volunteer steering committee, supported by a local part-time paid coordinator and a telephone *kiruv* trainer and coach. Their goal is to work with the community's shuls, organizations and individuals to raise the level of *kiruv* activity and awareness. This program is already in full swing in a number of communities across North America, including Passaic, Monsey, Toronto, Los Angeles, Cleveland, Baltimore and Denver. Local showings of "Inspired" and "Inspired Too" are often an effective launching point that blossom into full-scale community-wide programs.

It should be stressed that "coordinating" does not mean single-handedly organizing and directing every program. It only means channeling resources and keeping tabs on the programs, which may be run by others in the shul.

Most importantly, Project Inspire conducts *kiruv* training programs in locations throughout the country. Get things set up and you can have them come to you, too!

To keep information and inspiration flowing, Project Inspire intends to publish a monthly newsletter filled with *kiruv* tips, resources and success stories to give *chizuk*. They hope to also be able to customize it for each community.

Project Inspire already has an extensive list of books and websites that are ideally suited for Jews who are just beginning their journey in Torah learning.

Project Inspire's E-mail Box

Here is what some of Project Inspire's participants have to say about their experiences:

From: DW

Rabbi Sampson,

It's my pleasure to let you know just how big of a difference you make in people's lives. I was always "involved" in *kiruv*...[but] I never had the resources. Project Inspire basically hands you the best tools to get to someone's heart and soul. For example, I keep in my pocket the bookmarks or little pamphlets I get from Project Inspire. They come in handy at the weirdest moments. If you're on the train, or shopping or wherever, you can always pull them out and give them to people, and believe me, I did and still do.

Also, I attend college where there are many religious and non-religious Jews...I gave out [your] *mishlo'ach manos* with the story of Purim, and of course an invitation for Shabbos. I got many different responses. Most [people] were truly touched; I asked them for nothing in return and gave them a holiday gift...Then I went to the mall and gave some people *mishlo'ach manos* there. I got many phone calls and try to keep up with all of them. We sometimes learn together; it can be halachos or just schmoozing about the world or nothing in particular.

My family has an open invitation policy, so *baruch*

Hashem our Shabbos table looks really beautiful. We have people from all walks of life coming, staying for the whole Shabbos or just for a meal...It's amazing to see just how much people want to know about who they are and where they come from, and *b'emes* you guys make it all possible... I get many positive responses [to Project Inspire materials], and I know my sister does as well... We even got some people to enroll their children or themselves (depending on the age) in Oorah's summer camp! And the aish.com minute movies are the cutest — I enjoy them and forward them to as many souls as possible.

Im yirtzeh Hashem, I will keep you posted on the progress of all the goodness you are doing! And may Hashem grant you the *ko'ach* to continue with your avodas kodesh.

Good *yom tov* again,
DW

From: MA
Subject: Thank you!

Rabbi Sampson,

Thank you so much for organizing the Purim cards and informative fliers. My family distributed them with their *shalach manot*. My sister sent them to all her secular siblings-in-law, and to her parents-in-law and Conservative work colleagues, and my brother sent them to secular neighbors in his community... My father used them as a *kiruv* tool [by] distributing

Project Inspire

them with Hamantashen to Jewish colleagues and students. People were blown away and SO appreciative. What a meaningful Purim [we had by] giving *shalach manot* with inspiring messages to people who otherwise would pass over Purim without a thought!

Usually Purim was about giving another package to a family who had too much already to get rid of before Pesach. The recipients this year actually were touched and inspired.

I also personally mailed out *shalach manot* to old colleagues and acquaintances (from the gym, tennis...) that I've stayed in contact with via e-mail, etc. One such woman called me up on Purim crying that this was her first *shalach manot* ever! She proceeded to open it up and read aloud about each item in the basket. Then she excitedly unrolled the Purim explanation written on the scroll and wanted to read it aloud in order to discuss Purim and its significance. She was so moved that she finally allowed me to set her up with a learning partner to learn Torah weekly. What I'd been encouraging for over two years was accomplished with a simple *shalach manot* and cute Purim shpiel. She later told me that she called her secular daughter who was visiting in Israel to read her the Purim explanation as well.

Rabbi Sampson, I really wanted to thank you for all your hard work in "waking up" the *pintele neshamah* in Jews in our lives. The e-mails, calls and little seminars made me more aware of how to reach out in more interesting, creative and fun ways to the Jews in my life.

Yasher ko'ach for your hard work and please keep me informed of other projects so I can continue to try to inspire people around me...because that's what keeps me inspired too!

Chag kasher v'sameach,
MA

From: D
Subject: Something Exciting for Your Seder table!

Yasher ko'ach on the "4 Questions and 2 Jokes" kits. First some background... I work at a company that is very focused on "diversity." I've found it VERY uncomfortable to do any *kiruv* at work, invite anyone for Shabbos, etc. Anyhow, since most people do some sort of Seder for Pesach, even if it unfortunately includes bread and non-kosher food, the "4 Questions Kit" is very non-threatening. On *motzei Shabbos* I picked up a few extra "4 Questions Kits" to give to people at work. I just stopped by and dropped off a few copies in the offices of some co-workers and was surprised at the positive response. The people I gave them to were very grateful. One of them suggested I give a kit to a contractor who just started a couple days ago, who I didn't know was Jewish. Looks like I'll be picking up a few more at Mincha today.:)

— D

How to Get Involved

Project Inspire Manager: Cecilia Feiman
212-579-1388 ext 33
E-mail: projectinspire@aish.com

Director: Rabbi Chaim Sampson
212-579-1388 ext 21
csampson@aish.com

Or log on to: www.projectinspireonline.com

Chapter 10
THE VISION

Now that you've had a chance to learn the basic nuts and bolts of *kiruv*, it is time to "see things as they could be." So many people have made a difference, and you can, too. We must act effectively, and to do that, we need a vision.

It's Shabbos morning, and as you walk into shul, several members of the shul are accompanied by people who appear a little out of their element. During davening, you see that your fellow shul members are occasionally leaning over to their companions, showing them the correct page in the siddur or whispering brief explanations. At a *kiddush* following davening, each of the guests is warmly greeted by everyone they encounter.

Later that day, your shul sponsors a fascinating *shiur* attended by all these newcomers, as well as their hosts. It touches on a fundamental question that you've actually never thought much about: Why do Jews keep Shabbos?

The Vision

Amazingly, it's not just your shul where these activities are going on. It's happening in shuls, schools, *kollels* and homes all over your community, and in communities all over the country. And it's not just happening this week. It happens every week. And it doesn't only happen on Shabbos. Every day, newcomers to Torah are coming to night *seder* to learn with *yeshiva bachurim*. Religious women are hosting lunch-and-learn programs for their neighbors. Religious professionals are sponsoring similar events for their non-religious colleagues. This year, thousands of Jews who have never sat in a sukkah before find themselves the recipients of a dozen invitations. The flow of kindness, Torah and warmth between the religious and non-religious communities is now a surging river, and it is quickly carrying more and more unaffiliated Jews back to their heritage.

This fantasy is the realistic actualization of the book you have just read. It is the world we dare to envision, and we urge everyone who reads this book to choose at least one *kiruv* project — no matter how simple — to try. That alone would go a long way toward making our vision a reality.

All of the programs and ideas in this book are just waiting for you to get started. Now all we need are thousands of people to make a commitment. All you need do is count yourself in and you will succeed. It's guaranteed. Connect your fellow Jews to *Yiddishkeit* and they can only benefit. You can only benefit. If enough people respond to our call, the benefit to *Klal*

Yisrael will be incalculable.

Countless *kiruv* professionals have seen with their own eyes that the vast majority of people do not begin their quest for Judaism because of something they learn. Rather, it happens because of someone who influences them — someone who cares enough about them to share the most precious thing they have: their relationship with Hashem and knowledge of His Torah, our blueprint for life.

That someone can be you!

P.S. If you need help organizing your shul or group to make this vision a reality, feel free to e-mail me. I will do my best to assist you! You can reach me at: AharonUngar@gmail.com.

Chapter 11
CONCLUSION

The most powerful advertising in the world is word of mouth. If your rave reviews can succeed in getting someone to try a new restaurant or buy a new CD, they can convince someone to try one Shabbos or listen to one fantastic speaker on tape.

When you are aware of where that one experience can lead, you'll find yourself pouring your utmost efforts into selling it. Consider this true story: A woman who lives in Florida used to wear a gold necklace to work. The necklace was a gift from her children, and it said "*Ima*" in Hebrew. A co-worker once asked her about the lettering, and through the conversation that ensued, it became apparent that this woman was also Jewish. This conversation led to another conversation, which led to Shabbos invitations, which led to classes and more classes. Today, this co-worker is fully observant, married to a religious young man and living in Israel.

These things really happen, but they could happen on a far wider basis if, rather than waiting for random events to open doors, we proactively initiate interactions. The key lies within us; we must nurture within ourselves a love and enthusiasm for *Yiddishkeit* that will be contagious.

Go Slow

Even if someone does respond, remember that becoming religious is a long process. My father, Rabbi Cantor Robert Ungar, *z"l*, a *kiruv* pioneer in Atlanta, Georgia, in the 1960s, observed that those who leap into *Yiddishkeit* and seem to become religious overnight usually jump out just as quickly. They change so suddenly and completely that one day they wake up and do not recognize themselves. They begin to doubt the validity of what they have done, thinking it was some subtle form of temporary insanity. Soon they give it all up. In that light, you can understand why slow progress is in fact a very positive sign indicating healthy, lasting change. Don't be afraid to tell someone to slow down and not to take on too much at once!

New Name Needed

This brings us to another issue. How do we identify a person who is somewhere on the road between completely unaffiliated and firmly committed to Torah and mitzvos? Rabbi Mordecai Rottman posits that we need a new vocabulary — a positive, caring, motivational term that will make these returning Jews feel valued and accepted, even if they've only taken on one mitzvah. Someone who is learning, trying and taking small steps toward mitzvah observance is no longer what one would call unaffiliated or secular. Nor is he yet *frum*, or observant, but his steps forward are surely precious from Heaven's perspective. What we call him expresses how we view him, and in the new era we envision this word will be a frequently used one that will identify thousands of inspired Jews who are on their way home. If you have an idea for an appropriate term, please let me know.

How Do We View Them?

Probably one of the most powerful paragraphs ever written regarding a *frum* person trying to *mekarev* his non-*frum* brethren, is found at the conclusion to the "Twelfth *Middah* of Mercy" as described by the sacred kabbalist, Rabbi Moshe Cordevero, *zt"l*, in his *sefer Tomer Devorah*. His words open doors of light and set, in a most tangible and practical way, the internal foundation to enable a *frum* Jew to do *kiruv* successfully:

> So should a person be: even if he meets people who are against keeping Torah, he shall not act with cruelty against them, or belittle them and the like. Rather... he should say [to himself]: "After all, they are the children of Avraham, Yitzchak and Yaakov; if they are not [acting] kosher, their forefathers were kosher."

Always remember: True *kiruv* begins when one can arouse his inner feelings toward viewing all Jews (regardless of level of observance) as children of Avraham, Yitzchak and Yaakov. When he finds it in himself, in a real way, to feel this in his heart, the people he comes in contact with will feel it as well.

Difficulties

Certainly, as masses of Jews begin making efforts in *kiruv*, there will be a learning curve that we will have to successfully negotiate as *kiruv* becomes an integral part of our world. These will be "good" problems, because they represent a living, thriving *kiruv* movement that has been embraced by a wide swath of Torah Jews throughout the country. A far bigger problem — in truth, a tragedy — would be our failure to seize this moment in our history.

According to the Difficulty Is the Reward

I would like to leave you with the following thought as we conclude this *sefer*. The *Chovos Halevavos* says in "Gate of Love of Hashem," chapter 6, that it is important to be aware that the merits and the reward of one who brings another Jew closer to Torah and Hashem, so that he turns away from evil and toward the service of *Hakadosh Baruch Hu*, is even greater than one who has achieved the perfection of his soul in his devotion to Hashem and is even greater than one whose praiseworthy conduct, *middos*, *hishtadlus* and *ahavas Hashem* approaches the level of the prophets.

Get started.

Stop thinking, stop worrying, stop procrastinating…you can do it!

Chazak ve'ematz!

A PUBLIC CALL TO THE JEWISH PEOPLE

"Hear the word of Hashem, you who tremble at His word."
(Yeshayahu 66:5)

The situation of our brethren in the Land of Israel and the Diaspora is rapidly deteriorating. Inciters from both within and without are doing everything possible to uproot the Holy Torah and pure faith from our fellow Jews, leading them astray through seductive and false ideas. A DEVASTATING SPIRITUAL HOLOCAUST IS CLAIMING THE SOULS OF MILLIONS OF JEWS, WHO ARE ASSIMILATING AMONG THE GENTILES (may Hashem protect us).

We must not be silent at this hour. Rather, we must fortify ourselves, and learn and teach others how to draw hearts closer to Torah. As the Chofetz Chaim wrote: When one sees people drowning and doesn't know how to save them, he must hire people who do know how, or learn how himself!

We therefore proclaim that A HOLY OBLIGATION RESTS UPON EACH AND EVERY JEW TO DEVOTE HIS ENERGIES AND MONEY TO KIRUV RECHOKIM, through learning, teaching, and financially supporting those already involved in this holy work. Except for full-time students of Torah, who strengthen the Jewish people and prevent them from falling (G-d forbid), ABSOLUTELY NO ONE IS EXEMPT. We have personally witnessed the tremendous success of those active in this field who have saved tens of thousands of Jews from spiritual destruction. Most of the Jewish people are still wandering in the darkness, however, and it rests upon us to bring them into the light.

In the merit of this mitzvah, may Hashem hasten our Redemption and our salvation, and send us speedily Eliyahu HaNovi. May we see the fulfillment of the verse: "He shall return the hearts of parents to children and the hearts of children to their parents." And may we merit to see the coming of Moshiach Tzidkeinu speedily in our days, Amen.

Signed for the honor of the Holy One Blessed Be He and His Torah,

HaRav HaGaon Shmuel
Berenbaum

HaRav HaGaon
Mattisyahu Chaim Salomon

HaRav HaGaon Yaakov Perlow

HaRav HaGaon Aaron
Moshe Shechter

I add my voice HaRav HaGaon
Yosef Shalom Elyashiv

HaRav HaGaon Aharon
Leib Steinman

Appendix
KIRUV RESOURCES

KIRUV BOOKS

Beyond a Reasonable Doubt: Convincing Evidence of the Truths of Judaism, by Rabbi Shmuel Waldman (Feldheim).

Discover: Answers for Teenagers (and Adults) To Questions About the Jewish Faith, by Rabbi Dov Moshe Lipman (Feldheim).

The Eye of a Needle: Aish HaTorah's Kiruv Primer, compiled by Rabbi Yitzchak Coopersmith (Targum Press).

First Steps in Kiruv: A Few Basics for the Complete Novice, by Rabbi Dovid Abenson with Henye Meyer (Targum Press).

Jewish Matters: A Pocketbook of Knowledge and Inspiration, Edited by Rabbi Doron Kornbluth (Targum Press).

The Kiruv Files, by Rabbis Dovid Kaplan and Elimelech Meisels (Targum Press).

Light at the End of the Tunnel, an inspirational story by Rabbi Abraham J. Twerski, M.D. (Shaar Press).

Permission to Believe: Four Rational Approaches to G-d's Existence, by Rabbi Lawrence Kelemen (Targum Press).

Permission to Receive: Four Rational Approaches to the Torah's Divine Origin, by Rabbi Lawrence Kelemen (Targum Press).

Questions You Thought We Were Afraid You'd Ask and Answers You've Been Waiting to Hear, by Moshe Speiser (Targum Press).

Reaching Out, by Rabbi Aryeh Kaplan (NCSY/OU), available from ArtScroll.

What Do You Mean, You Can't Eat in My Home? A Guide to How Newly Observant Jews and Their Less-Observant Relatives Can Still Get Along, by Azriela Jaffe (Schocken Books).

Why Marry Jewish? Surprising Reasons for Jews to Marry Jews by Rabbi Doron Kornbluth (Targum Press).

RECOMMENDED WEBSITES FOR LEARNING AND DOING KIRUV

Kiruv Training and Resources:

www.AJOP.com
www.eKiruv.org

Appendix

www.Kiruv.com
www.NerLeElef.com
www.NerLeElef.org
www.NJOP.org
www.OzNidberu.org

Project Inspire:

www.InspireJews.com
www.KiruvUSA.com
www.ProjectInspireOnline.com

Anti-Missionary:

www.JewsForJudaism.org
www.OutreachJudaism.org

Other:

www.TorahLab.org
www.DiscoveryProduction.com

RECOMMENDED WEBSITES FOR BEGINNERS

Classes and Lectures:

www.AishAudio.com
www.AishCafe.com
www.ClassicSinai.com
www.DovidGottlieb.com
www.EnglishTorahTapes.com

www.JewishRenaissance.org
www.JewishStudies.org
www.Naaleh.com
www.ouRadio.org
www.RabbiLeff.net
www.ShemaYisrael.com
www.SimpleToRemember.com
www.TeachItToMe.com
www.TheShmuz.com
www.Torah.org
www.TorahMedia.com
www.YadAvraham.org
www.613.org

Essays and Articles:

www.Aish.com
www.ArachimUSA.org
www.BeingJewish.com
www.InnerNet.org.il
www.Isralight.org
www.Ohr.edu
www.SimpleToRemember.com

General Jewish Life:

www.ou.org

Intermarriage:

www.WhyDateJewish.com
www.WhyMarryJewish.com

Appendix

College Students:
www.JeffSeidel.com

Getting Answers:
www.AskTheRabbi.org (get answers to your questions, generally within 24 hours)
www.JewishAnswers.org (check the indexed archive of Q & A or submit your own)

Other:
www.AStillSmallVoice.org (Jewish correspondence school classes by mail)
www.ChadishMedia.com ("how to" tapes and CDs)
www.TorahToday.com (one-minute, daily, e-mail streaming audio Torah messages)

ELECTRONIC MEDIA

Real Questions...Real Answers: Answers to the Most Frequently Asked Questions About Judaism, 6 CD-ROM Set (Windows Only) with answers from Rav Shmuel Kamenetsky, Rav Noach Weinberg, Rav Mordechai Becher, Rav Beryl Gershenfeld, Rav Reuven Leuchter, Rav Yerachmiel Milstein and more...Published by the Association for Jewish Outreach Programs (AJOP), available from ArtScroll

FREE RESOURCES AND SERVICES:

Free Kiruv Hotline sponsored by Oz Nidberu for questions related to *kiruv*: 1-800-98 KIRUV

Free Phone Chavrusa for beginners:
www.PartnersInTorah.org

Free Private Lessons offered in your home:
www.GotTorah.com

Request Free Tefillin:
www.TefillinBank.com

Free Books for Use in Kiruv:
Beyond a Reasonable Doubt: Convincing Evidence of the Truths of Judaism, by Rabbi Shmuel Waldman. Available from www.SimpleToRemember.com/vitals/free-jewish-book.htm.

Why Marry Jewish? Surprising Reasons for Jews to Marry Jews, by Rabbi Doron Kornbluth. Available from www.SimpleToRemember.com/vitals/free-jewish-book.htm.

LEADING USA KIRUV ORGANIZATIONS

(Partial List)

AFIKIM FOUNDATION
111 John Street, Suite 1720
New York, NY 10038
Phone: 212-791-7450
www.AfikimFoundation.org

Afikim was established to attend to the critical challenges of our day by developing creative initiatives in the areas of Torah, *mesorah*, *zikaron* and *chessed*.

AISH HATORAH
One Western Wall Plaza
POB 14149
Old City, Jerusalem 91141 ISRAEL
Phone: +972 (0) 525 44 85 44 (Israel)
+1 917 558 6837 (USA)
+ 44 (0) 7974 224 720 (UK)
www.vocaishion.com
www.kiruv.com

Aish HaTorah is a world leader in creative Jewish educational programs and leadership training, dedicated to answering the vital question, "Why be Jewish?" Founded in Jerusalem by Rav Noach Weinberg in 1974, Aish HaTorah is dedicated to revitalizing the Jewish people by providing opportunities for Jews of all backgrounds to discover their heritage in an atmosphere of open inquiry and mutual respect. Aish HaTorah operates 26 full-time branches on five continents. Aish.com receives over 2.5 million visits each month.

ASSOCIATION FOR JEWISH OUTREACH PROGRAMS (AJOP)
1705 Reisterstown Road
Baltimore MD 21208
Phone: 410-653-AJOP (2567)
E-mail: ruchama@ajop.com
www.ajop.org

AJOP is an independent network that supports the men and women who have dedicated their lives to guiding Jews to a life enriched by traditional Torah values. AJOP recognizes that the critical role played by these outreach specialists provides a significant counterforce to the wave of assimilation sweeping our people. The organization supports the growth of new outreach programs, helps existing outreach programs expand and facilitates new initiatives to respond to new challenges in outreach and inreach as they arise. It supports, serves and enhances the skills of outreach workers throughout the world.

DISCOVERY SEMINARS
(Division of Aish HaTorah)
POB 14149
70 Misgav Ladach Street
Jewish Quarter, Jerusalem 91141
Phone: (972-2) 627-7742
E-mail: discoveryisrael@aish.com
www.aish.com/discoveryisrael/index.html

With its crisp, entertaining style, Discovery uses scientific methods to explore the authenticity of Judaism and its relevance today. It debunks popular misconceptions about Judaism and answers the question: "Why be Jewish?" Discovery is known worldwide for its presentation of "Bible Codes." Over 100,000 people on five continents have "done Discovery."

ENCOUNTER USA
Rabbi Yisroel Roll, Director
6204 Cross Country Blvd, Suite 318
Baltimore, Maryland 21215
Phone: 410-585 1138
E-mail: yisroelhillel@aol.com
www.EncounterUSA.com

Encounter develops diverse educational and social

Appendix

programs that are marketed in a non-traditional manner to unaffiliated and marginally affiliated Jews. Their goal is to offer Jews from all backgrounds and levels the opportunity to re-connect with their faith in a non-pressured and open environment. All Encounter programs and events offer participants an entree into the world of Judaism, its history and its observances.

GATEWAYS
Main Office:
11 Wallenberg Circle
Monsey, NY 10952
Phone: 800-722-3191 — 845-352-0393
E-mail: office@gatewaysonline.com
www.GatewaysOnline.org

HASHEVAYNU
144-02 Jewel Ave, 2nd Floor
Kew Gardens Hills, NY 11367
Phone: 718-275-2200
E-mail: info@hashevaynu.org

Dedicated to helping *baalei teshuvah* settle into the New York Jewish community and maintain their Torah way of life following a *kiruv* program or yeshiva.

JERUSALEM FELLOWSHIPS
119 W. 72nd St., New York, NY 10023
Phone: 1-800 FELLOWS 212-909-2709
E-mail: jf@aish.com
www.GoIsrael.org

There is no place in the world like Israel and there is no better way to experience Israel than on Aish Jerusalem

Fellowships Programs. Combining fun, adventure and education, Aish Jerusalem Fellowships has been organizing trips to Israel for 20 years and currently brings over 2,000 students annually to Israel from around the world. Check out their various programs, from introductory to more advanced, to find the program that will best suit your need to have an inspiring trip to Israel. Or join their adventures around the world. Trips to Europe, South America and within the United States are offered to students from various campuses. All programs combine fun, adventure and education in a unique way. Explore exciting locations such as London, Prague and New York City while also exploring the depths of Judaism. Trips vary in length and costs.

LEGACY RETREATS
Monsey, NY
Phone: (845) 425-1370
Elisha Finman, Director 718-614-7649
E-mail: unrabbi@legacyretreats.org
www.LegacyRetreats.org

For over a decade thousands of college students and young professionals have been empowered by Legacy Retreats to explore and embrace their rich Jewish heritage. Students come from Ivy League universities and colleges from across North America to explore the basis of Judaism's core beliefs. Their serene 10-acre campus and *beis midrash* environment provides a state-of-the-art facility located in the heart of Monsey, a beautiful suburb of New York.

NATIONAL CONFERENCE OF SYNAGOGUE YOUTH (NCSY)
11 Broadway
New York, NY 10004
Phone: (212) 613-8233
E-mail: ncsy@ou.org
www.ncsy.org

NCSY may be the most effective and respected educational Jewish youth movement in the world. Offering programs to bring Jewish teens back to their heritage, NCSY is at the forefront of the battle against assimilation. Although most of NCSY's effort have been in North America, now NCSY in Israel is trying to bring back Israeli teens to their roots as well. There are many hundreds of local NCSY chapters across America which offer educational and social events for Jewish teens.

NATIONAL JEWISH OUTREACH PROGRAM (NJOP)
989 6th Ave, 10th Floor
New York, NY 10018
Phone: 646-871-4444 1-800-44-HEBRE(W)

NJOP was founded in 1987 by Rabbi Ephraim Buchwald, in response to the urgent need to prevent the loss of Jews to Jewish life due to assimilation and lack of Jewish knowledge. NJOP has become one of the largest and most successful Jewish outreach organizations in the world by offering people positive, joyous, Jewish educational opportunities and experiences. NJOP currently sponsors free "Crash Courses" in Hebrew Reading, Basic Judaism and Jewish History, TURN FRIDAY NIGHT INTO SHABBAT, Beginners

Services, READ HEBREW AMERICA/CANADA and SHABBAT ACROSS AMERICA/CANADA, at more than 3,650* locations across North America, and in 35* countries worldwide. NJOP has successfully reached close to 983,000* North American Jews and engaged them in Jewish life. (*Figures as of 6/07.)

OORAH
1805 Swarthmore Avenue
Lakewood, NJ 08701
Phone: 732-730-1000 / 1-800-21-OORAH

Oorah, which means "Awaken," was founded in 1980 with the goal of awakening Jewish children and their families to their heritage. They seek out families who are interested in enriching their spiritual lives, and provide them with the right resources to succeed. In particular, they assist children to enroll in Jewish day schools, yeshivos and camps where they receive a full religious and secular education straight through high school. While the children learn and grow, Oorah brings adult education opportunities to the parents, as well as all the ritual objects and support they need to live a full Jewish life.

PARTNERS IN TORAH
www.PartnersInTorah.org or www.Study42.org
US and Canada: 1-800-STUDY-4-2 or 732-363-3330
E-mail: info@partnersintorah.org
England: 011-44 8000 JLEARN (553-276)
www.phoneandlearn.org
Israel: 02-652-0114 or 052-763-4743 (cell)

Partners in Torah matches Jewish adults who want

to know more about their heritage with a friendly, knowledgeable mentor for an hour a week of Jewish study and discussion by phone. Connect with over 3,000 years of Jewish wisdom cost-free. (They even pay for the phone calls!)

PROJECT GENESIS
122 Slade Avenue, Suite 250
Baltimore, MD 21208
Phone 888-WWW-TORA(H) or (410) 602-1350
E-mail: genesis@torah.org

Project Genesis leverages new technology to engage Jews worldwide in Jewish educational programming. In functional terms, Project Genesis is the IT department for Jewish outreach.

Torah.org reaches out to Jews by providing quality Jewish classes and resources.

JewishAnswers.org opens itself to the questions and concerns of our readership, provides answers from Rabbis around the globe and seeks to further the Jewish education of the Jews who are asking for more. The Torah Forum engages participants in ongoing, threaded discussions of Jewish topics.

eKiruv.com helps those devoted to Jewish outreach to carry out their missions more effectively.

TorahMedia.com channels thousands of recordings of Jewish content from Jewish educators to those thirsty for Jewish knowledge.

Additional services include free Web and e-mail hosting for Jewish outreach organizations, e-mail discussion lists for outreach and technology advice and tips to help Rabbis and leaders reach out to our fellow Jews, both on-line and off.

PROJECT GESHER
Director: Rabbi Aaron Gruman
Contact: Rabbi Ezriel Munk
E-mail: info@ProjectGesher.org
Phone: 732-367-0600

A division of Beis Midrash Govoha (Lakewood Yeshiva), it offers over 1,600 trained people working at over 64 sites in the Tri-State area. Gesher sends personnel beyond the Tri-State area on an as-needed basis. Gesher works together with local Rabbis and communities to provide one-on-one study *chavrusos*, Shabbos invitations, *shiurim* and back-up materials.

ABOUT THE AUTHOR

Since making aliyah four years ago, Aharon Ungar has been learning full-time in *kollel*. First in Yeshivas Toras Moshe, under Rav Moshe Meiselman, *shlita*, and then in Yeshivas HaRan, both in Yerushalayim.

Aharon Ungar's hands-on experience in *kiruv* includes private tutoring of *baalei teshuvah* and *geirim* and initiating and leading beginner's minyanim, in conjunction with the National Jewish Outreach Program (NJOP).

Mr. Ungar grew up in Atlanta, Georgia. After graduating Yeshiva University magna cum laude, he went on to earn an M.B.A. in Marketing from New York University's Stern Graduate School of Business. His professional positions were primarily in the area of marketing and sales until he and his wife, Jennifer, founded Diabetic.com in Florida in 1993.

Mr. Ungar co-founded and learned in the Boca Raton Community Kollel and, later after moving to Miami Beach, maintained his nightly *seder* at the Lakewood Kollel.

In 2002, Aharon and Jennifer sold the company and retired to Israel. They currently reside in Ramat Beit Shemesh with their six children, *keneina hara*, Nachum, Yaakov Aryeh, Ariella Tzipora, Akiva Baruch, Esther Tzirel and Yael Bracha.

YOU'VE read the book.
BE A PART OF THIS IMPORTANT MOMENT FOR KLAL YISRAEL.

Help us create more tools like this
to help bring Jews closer to Torah.

PLEASE TAKE 5 MINUTES...

Complete this quick survey about the book, or use the link below.
YOUR opinion is important to us!

PUTTING OUT THE FIRE READERS' SURVEY

If you do not have enough space to write your answers here, please continue on another piece of paper.

1. What topic in *Putting Out the Fire* was most interesting to you?

_____

2. What topic was the most practical for you?

_____

3. What aspects of *kiruv* would you like to learn more about?

_____

4. What could we provide to make doing *kiruv* easier for you?

_____

5. Which of the 99 ideas in the book are you going to try?

_____

6. Do you have any ideas for what people can do to reach out to other Jews that you want me to include in the next book?

_____

7. If we set up a free online social network for people involved with *kiruv*, both lay people and professionals, to share ideas, expertise and resources, would you participate regularly?

For updates on Putting Out the Fire and future publications, or if you would like to help us create more books like this by taking our online survey, go to www.targum.com/kiruv-books-info.html
or e-mail us at: kiruvinfo@targum.com

8. What would you like me to write about in the next book?
_____

9. What are the two questions you are most often asked by non-*frum* people about *Yiddishkeit*?
_____

10. If you are already making some effort at *kiruv*, what's working for you? What's hardest? What's easiest?
_____

11. If you are not doing *kiruv* yet, why not?
_____

12. What would you say to somebody to convince them to get involved with *kiruv*?
_____

13. Do you have a *kiruv* story of your own you want to share?
_____

PLEASE INCLUDE YOUR CONTACT INFORMATION BELOW TO RECEIVE UPDATES ON PUTTING OUT THE FIRE AND FUTURE PUBLICATIONS:

First Name_____ Last Name_____
Address_____City_____
State _____ Country_____
Zip _____ Tel #_____
E-mail_____

____Yes! I would like to receive updates about Putting Out the Fire, future publications or other books on Jewish outreach.
____Yes! I would like to receive e-mails from Targum Press for online updates, offers and giveaways and everyday 10% off discounts at www.targum.com.

Mail or fax to: Targum Press, Inc.
In U.S. 22700 W. Eleven Mile Rd., Southfield, MI 48034
Fax: 888-298-9992, or in ISRAEL: POB 43170, Jerusalem, Israel, 91430
Tel: 02-651-3355 / Fax: 02-651-0342 or at www.targum.com
E-mail: kiruvinfo@targum.com